Phantoms of Chittagong

The "Fifth Army" in Bangladesh

Phantoms of Chittagong
The "Fifth Army" in Bangladesh

MAJOR GENERAL S.S. UBAN (RETD.)
PVSM, AVSM

ALLIED PUBLISHERS PVT. LTD.

Noida • Mumbai • Kolkata • Chennai • Bangalore

Contents

This book is dedicated to the gallant officers and men of the SPECIAL FRONTIER FORCE, who made the supreme sacrifice of their lives, braving dangers beyond the call of their duty and blazing immortal trails in the history of righteous wars waged against oppression and for the freedom of all mankind.

Foreword

Major General S.S. Uban, the author and hero of this book, is a unique personality—an amalgam of spirituality and a burning zeal to defend the values which sustain a civilised society. A winner of the two of the highest Indian decorations for gallantry in war, he is also admirable constructive worker for rural development at grassroots level.

All three of our esteemed Prime Ministers have showered high praise on him. Pandit Jawaharlal Nehru while congratulating him on one of his daring exploits, once said: *"We are proud of you."* Mrs. Indira Gandhi, while congratulating him on his unprecedented victories with small commando forces in the Bangladesh War, said: *"You were the backbone of all our successes in the Bangladesh War."* Mr. R.N. Kao, under whom the Special Frontier Force worked with such distinction, called him *"a living legendary figure"* in his farewell speech. More recently, Shri Rajiv Gandhi in a message has appreciated Major General Uban's efforts in opening a rural charitable hospital in the west Himalayan foothills and blessed the venture.

The late Sheikh Mujeebur Rehman, the then President of Bangladesh, requested late Prime Minister Mrs. India Gandhi to send Major General Uban to him as his Personal Adviser. During a short period in that capacity, the Major General developed a remarkable rapport with Sheikh Mujeebur Rehman who treated him as a member of his own family. Major General Uban played a notable role in smoothening relations between Bangladesh and Pakistan on the one hand and strengthening their ties with India on the other.

His military exploits in the Chittagong Hill Tracts with an unbelievable small force of Guerillas earned for the Special Frontier Force (SFF) the title of "Phantoms of Chittagong". Field Marshal Manekshaw called this small force "The Fifth Army". The goals undertaken and the daring tactics employed excite one's admiration. These will no doubt be studied by Military Commanders with great interest. This book was overdue. There was consternation in Pakistan about what was happening in the Chittagong Hill Tracts during the War. Very few people know how the most dangerous flank of the Army's IVth Corps was secured and kept safe during the entire operation. This book will amply clear the position. It would not be exaggeration to say that the Special Frontier Force greatly helped the Pakistani Military leadership to make up their minds to surrender to the Indian Army, since their only escape route across the Arakan Road into Burma or possibly to the safety of the Seventh American Fleet was cut off by the Special Frontier Force, at a very short notice, by blowing up the Dohazari bridge. The most amazing part of this narration by Major General Uban is the unbelievable meager resources in men and material with which he was able to achieve such outstanding results, on the sheer strength of his fearless personality. His officers and men performed herculean tasks at his bidding.

The Major General was fighting two wars—one through the professionally trained soldiers in the Chittagong Hill Tracts and the other through the Bangladeshi patriots who had been trained and organised by him into a force called the "Mujeeb Bahini" and who were fighting throughout Bangladesh. These men adored him for his total involvement in their cause.

I can say with confidence that the heroic exploits of the Special Frontier Force under the charismatic leadership of Major General S.S. Uban will rank with some of the best of their kind anywhere in the world.

After his retirement, Major General Uban joined the World Conference of Religion for Peace and was elected its first Secretary General in India. In this capacity, he put new life into the movement of peace through religion and, working tirelessly, he opened over 30 multi-religious chapters of this organisation throughout India—all working for communal harmony and peace. He led memorable Peace marches in Punjab and held several conventions of Punjabi leaders in Delhi and Chandigarh. He was also appointed as the Associate Secretary General of Asian Conference on Religion and Peace, and Secretary of its Reconciliation Commission. He is also the author of the now famous book, *The Gurus of India,* in which he describes his personal experiences with the Spiritual Masters of various faiths. His conclusion is that all faiths, howsoever different in their approach, lead to the one and the only God. He has numerous admirers of all faiths throughout the world. Recently, he has founded a "Vanguard for Peace Foundation" with the sole aim of rejuvenating rural society by scientific and spiritual orientation. A Destitute Children's Home and the Onkarnath Charitable Hospital in the rural area of the west Himalayan foothills are two of his recent achievements in the cause of suffering humanity.

He is Mother India's true soldier indeed.

GOPAL SINGH
Lt-Governor
Goa, Daman and Diu
and
Administrator
Dadra and Nagar Haveli

Cabo Raj Niwas
Dona Paula
Goa 408 004
15 August, 1985

CHAPTER 1

Prelude to Revolt

The origin of the idea of constituting the Muslim majority areas of India into a new nation called Pakistan was based, it is assumed, on hatred and mistrust of the Hindus who were in a majority, by some fanatic and power-hungry Muslim leaders. This assumption can only be partially true. What ultimately led to the partition of our common motherland was the frantic desire of the British rulers, who saw no scope of getting any foothold, economic or otherwise, in an independent Hindu India. They felt certain, however, that Muslim Pakistan would eternally remain tied to their apron strings, being a smaller country lacking in the requisite resources.

The British have followed the same pattern in all the countries which they were forced to leave. The Republic of Ireland is a typical example besides many others.

Thus, a massive campaign of hatred between the Hindus and the Muslims was engineered by interested parties, who made sure that no scheme, which could keep the whole of India united, was ever allowed to fructify. The result was the partition of the country, not on economic, geographical or historical grounds but on the basis of religion. This was despite the fact that a vast majority of Muslims who were going to form a separate nation came from the same racial stock, spoke the same language and inherited the same history and geography. Religion, which should be a uniting force, was used as the only powerful argument for separation, and the British, the sole beneficiary and arbitrator, accepted it. The very name 'Pakistan' signified perpetual enmity. Pakistan means "Land of the Pure" (Muslims), which implied that what they were leaving behind was impure (*Napak*). It was only much later that even Mr M.A. Jinnah, the architect of Pakistan, realised that they were only getting a moth-eaten country and had lost greatly in the deal.

Punjabi Muslims and the Bengali Muslims who were to form the real base of Pakistan suffered more losses than others. But fanaticism won the day and the communal frenzy took a serious turn.

Communal mobs were incited to kill the minority communities on both sides of the arbitrary dividing line, which was yet to be drawn. Thousands of innocent men, women and children were butchered and hundreds of thousands rendered homeless and shoved into refugee camps. This part is too painful to recount. The author personally saw hundreds of Hindu dead bodies in the Peshawar Cantonment Police Station and Muslim dead bodies along the railway lines in East Punjab. Police, and even Army units, used weapons against their erstwhile neighbours and friends. As a result of this unprecedented orgy of violence, even men like Jawahar Lal Nehru and Sardar Patel felt reconciled to the division of the country although they never accepted the so-called Two-Nation Theory with religion as the basis of Nationalism.

Hindus, by and large, were comparatively prosperous, and while leaving their ancestral homes in Pakistan, were looted and left only in the clothes they happened to be wearing, when they were made to run for their lives. But the poor Muslims who had high hopes of occupying Hindu property got nothing. The already rich Khans and the officer class took over much of the loot. The Muslim refugees from India were given what was left. They were predominantly agricultural and industrial labour and Pakistan settled them on Hindu lands in Sind, depriving the poor Muslim peasantry of Sind of a chance to better their prospects.

This continues to bedevil the relations between the Pak Centre and the Sind Province. Sindhi Muslims were the first to suffer from the impact of the partition. They suffered more when the Pak military dictatorship resettled many Punjabi soldiers on the rich Sind land.

The same Punjabi domination was exercised in the Defence forces, the Police and even in Para-Military forces. Baluchistan, with unparalleled traditions of independence, was ravaged by Punjabi troops under General Tikka Khan who became notorious as the "Butcher of Baluchistan'. The techniques of torture against the civil population perfected in Baluchistan were later used in Bangladesh by the same

General Tikka Khan with disastrous results. The North West Frontier Province of the Valiant Pathans was already out of grace with the ruling junta for joining hands with the Indian National Congress to win Independence for the whole country. The astonishing thing was that the British lackeys of pre-Independence days became the rulers, by misleading Pak Muslims with the propaganda that the erstwhile freedom fighters of the stature of Khan Abdul Ghaffar Khan, Wali Khan and Khan Abdul Samad Khan were the stooges of Hindus and, therefore, could not safeguard Muslim interests.

The Woes of Bangladesh

Islam in Pakistan means the interests of Punjabi Muslims (still the sword-arm of that nation) and their allies in other provinces. Anyone else in Pakistan, who professes equal status, is an infidel. This philosophy was applicable, with much greater force, against the Bengali Muslims who were considered racially inferior and who had the further misfortune of being the majority community in Pakistan. The present Bangladesh, which constituted the Eastern Wing of Pakistan, was over a thousand miles away from its capital Islamabad or Karachi, the next most important port city, which further widened the gulf.

Bengali Muslims had high hopes of bettering their economic condition as a part of Pakistan for very cogent reasons. They constituted the majority and, in any democratic set up their very cohesive entity would entitle them to rule Pakistan. Their level of education and intelligence was also much higher as compared to other provinces of Pakistan. They were the main foreign-exchange earners through their jute and tea. In a democratic set up, they had everything in their favour. Some of them like Biharis in Bangladesh followed, nay even excelled, in mass Hindu killings started by West Pakistan, to prove their bonafides as true Muslims of Pakistan. But they failed to realise that their interests clashed with the Punjabis who wielded the real power through their Army.

With one stroke, the Punjabi politicians outwitted the astute Bengali. Urdu was declared the national language of Pakistan and the Bengali, consequently, found himself always at a disadvantage. The Bengali's majority was reduced by various constitutional formulae, each designed to progressively lower the status of Bengalis in all spheres. All this was, of course, under the pretext of the so-called Islamic interest as interpreted and understood in Islamabad. Bengali Muslims with their legalistic bent of mind felt completely disillusioned and sore and tried all constitutional methods but in vain.

Pak-style Democracy

Field Marshal Ayub Khan, the military dictator of Pakistan, proclaimed a constitution introducing what he called "basic democracies", where only 80,000 electors out of a population of one hundred million were allowed to vote for councils to be formed at different administrative levels. This ensured almost a permanent military dictatorship. But Bangladeshis were not to be cowed down by naked military power. They protested in 1962 and braved the repression unleashed particularly against the student community, who were spearheading the movement to re-establish civil rule and true democracy.

When the agitation grew very strong in 1965, Ayub ordered wanton and unprovoked aggression against India, in order to divert public attention. Unfortunately, the Pakistanis got badly trounced in this war, which gave further fillip to the movement for autonomy in East Pakistan. Bangladeshis further observed that their country was left defenceless in this war and but for the goodwill of India, it could have been easily overrun by the Indian Army.

Sheikh Mujeebur Rehman, who had become the unquestioned leader of this region and of the Awami League, announced his six-point demand, which essentially sought racial and economic autonomy. Ayub implicated Sheikh Mujeebur Rehman in the trumped up 'Agartala Conspiracy Case' and imprisoned thousands of his Awami League followers as traitors in 1968. The Pakistan Army and Police created a reign of terror which intensified the struggle of Bangladeshis for autonomy. Student and youth leaders like Fazal-ul-Haq Moni, Tufail, Abdul Razak, Shiraz and Rab raised hell, which forced Ayub to step down and hand over the power to General Yahya Khan, Commander-in-Chief of the Pakistan Army.

Yahya Khan knew from the very start that the days of military dictatorship were numbered. There were persistent demands even in West

Pakistan to restore democracy. Yahya Khan promised a return to democracy based on adult franchise and ordered elections in both wings (East and West Pakistan) on 7 December 1970. Mujeeb's Awami League fought the elections on their six-point demand of autonomy and won 160 out of 162 seats from East Bengal in the National Assembly consisting of 300 members. In the Western wing, Z.A. Bhutto, leading the Pakistani Peoples' Party, secured 87 out of 138 seats. It was obvious from the results that Mujeeb would be the future Prime Minister of Pakistan and the Bengali majority would get its programme of autonomy approved in the National Assembly. This was not acceptable to Islamabad.

Here Mr Z.A. Bhutto found himself in sharp conflict with Sheikh Mujeebur Rehman in his bid for total power. Sheikh Mujeeb was always for a federal Pakistan with each wing enjoying complete autonomy in the matter of every subject except Defence and Foreign Affairs. The Sheikh was also against calling it an Islamic Republic, having secular and modern views on statecraft. It suited Bhutto on the other hand to have a strong centre and Islam as the big stick to beat any opponents with. Bhutto threatened to boycott the Assembly unless Mujeeb relented on his six points. The Assembly session was, therefore, postponed, confirming the view in the Bengali mind that power would never be transferred to elected representatives of the people in Pakistan, in a peaceful manner.

CHAPTER 2

Volcano Erupts

Sheikh Mujeebur Rehman gave a call to his people for non-cooperation and a civil disobedience movement. The response was total. The Sheikh then nominated a Citizens, Administrative Council to take over charge from 1 March 1971.

President Yahya Khan came to Dacca to personally negotiate with Sheikh Mujeebur Rehman. The talks started on 16 March 1971 and went on for several days. Mr Bhutto also arrived to participate. Under this facade of negotiations, shiploads of Pakistani troops disembarked at Chittagong and Chalna to augment the already formidable force of about 60,000 troops in East Pakistan. As soon as the concentration and appropriate deployment of troops according to a well thought out plan was completed on 25 March 1971, negotiations were abruptly broken off. Yahya Khan's flight back to Karachi was the signal for the Army under General Tikka Khan to crush the popular movement in East Pakistan. Tikka Khan had won his spurs in this very line in Baluchistan. The 'Butcher of Baluchistan' set about his task with the throughness of a relentless and remorseless fanatic. Thousands of Bengali workers, who had refused to handle the Army supplies at Chittagong, were mowed down by machine-gun fire. A day prior to Yahya's departure from Dacca, and a reign of terror was let loose immediately after his departure.

Sheikh Mujeebur Rehman saw no other course open to himself under these circumstances, except to declare Bangladesh a sovereign Independent republic from 25 March 1971. President Yahya Khan charged Mujeeb with treason, clamped Martial Law and banned all political activities.

Students and intellectuals formed their selected targets for extinction. In Dacca University, hundreds of students and professors were shot down and many girl students kidnapped from the University Campus by the Pak Army. On 13 April 300 students of

St. Francis Xavier's School in Jessore were lined up and machine-gunned. The Parish Priest was also killed.

World Opinion

Mr Mort Rosenblum, the press correspondent of the Associated Press, after touring East Pakistan during this period, reported a civil war of staggering butchery and hatred. It was estimated that this civil war toll since 25 March exceeded the 4,00,000 deaths in this country during a cyclone in November.

In an earlier despatch from Bangkok, Mr Rosenblum wrote "Vultures too full to fly, perch along the Ganga River in grim contentment. They have had perhaps more than half a million murdered Pakistanis to feed upon since March."

The Sunday Telegraph of London said, "Whatever happens, the old Pakistan is dead. The rulers are trying to deny the fact by arms but the attempt cannot be other than tragic folly."

Pravda stated on 2 April 1971, "These (Pakistani) army actions are nothing other than crude arbitrariness and violence which arouses the serious concern of Soviet people."

The Guardian (27 March 1971) said, "The President's stance made Sheikh Mujeeb's reported declaration of Independence for Bengal inevitable. Bengal's secession means that the illogic of a united Pakistan—the hallowed Islamic inheritance from Mohammad Ali Jinnah has shown itself again. The miracle is that it lasted so long in spite of sporadic out-bursts of regional tensions."

The Daily Telegraph (27 March 1971) said. "The tragedy is that whatever the West Pakistan Army may do, at whatever terrible cost, to restore order now, it cannot create a stable and durable democratic system."

Then on 29 March 1971, the paper stated, "All the bayonets from West Punjab cannot shove back into the bottle "the genie of Bengali nationalism".

The Gaurdian (14 April 1971) said, "The United Nations will surely collapse in bitter laughter, if Kashmir comes up again. The issue is as dead as the students of Dacca University.

The New York Times of 28 March 1971 counselled a federal link between East and West Pakistan in preference to a policy of bloody repression.

The Washington Evening Star of 28 March 1971 acknowledged the state of a civil war in East Pakistan and issued a warning about the prospects of a peoples' war there.

A senior Republican Senator, Mr. William B. Saxbi, said, "I am distressed at the reported and actual killing and maiming of many people, most of them unarmed, and the severity of measures taken to repress the feelings there (Bangladesh)". He was distressed also that "Pakistanis were using American arms, given for self-defence, against their own people."

The French paper *L. Aurore* (28 March 1971) said that the "civil war in East Pakistan was to be expected ever since the cyclone, which made known to the world the contradictions of this country by giving them a tragic illustration." The newspaper further felt that "thousands of people might pay with their lives for the error committed in 1947 (Indian partition) and the obstinacy of the Pakistani military authorities."

Senator Edward Kennedy pointed out the special responsibility of the USA in East Bengal where "it is our military hardware, our guns, tanks and aircraft which are contributing to the sufferings (of people there) and this is being done in violation of negotiated agreements on the use of American military aid."

The Uhusan Malaysia of Kuala Lumpur said, "We do not enjoy blaming the leaders of West Pakistan but what we have clearly observed is that East Pakistan is, in fact, not a part of an Independent territory but a mere colony of West Pakistan… We consider Yahya Khan's present action a blunder."

Rising Nepal and *New Herald* of Kathmandu said that a point of no return had been reached. Thousands of East Pakistanis were sacrificing their lives and that disintegration would follow.

A mass circulation Japanese newspaper *Mainichi Shimbun* of Tokyo said, "Military oppression cannot solve the problem. Anybody can see that East Pakistani demand for self-determination and freedom from poverty will not be crushed by guns and swords.

The Zambian *Daily Mail* of Lusaka said, "President Yahya Khan should be persuaded against thinking that any permanent solution would come out of the barrel of a gun."

In an Istanbul daily, *Yeni Gazette*, Kikmat Bil said, "Pakistan never was one country. Now uninvited, Western tanks, planes, helicopters and the army was in Bengal. This uninvited army tries to keep the ties of the east in its hands. How long can this be possible?"

'*Yeni Istanbul, Gunaydi, Gumhuriyet, Ulus* all of Turkey', expressed fears about disintegration of Pakistan and condemned military repression.

Kayhan International of Teheran wrote, "As Awami League Leader Sheikh Mujeebur Rehman and his leading lieutenants begin yet another term of imprisonment, the stage seems set for fratricide on a large scale ... it is obvious that the problems of East Pakistan cannot be solved through the use of force."

Even the opinion of Turkish and Iranian allies had no effect on the Military regime in Pakistan. The world opinion was totally ignored.

Strangely enough, *China* was the only country in the whole wide world which supported the action of Pak Arms. On 14 April Peking Radio broadcast a commentary from the *Peoples, Daily* on a message sent by Prime Minister Chou en Lai to General Yahya Khan. It said:

> The relevant measures taken up by President Yahya Khan in connection with the present situation in Pakistan are the internal affairs of Pakistan. The Chinese Government and people will always vehemently support the Pakistan Government in its just struggle for safeguarding national independence and sovereignty.

China also sent a protest note to India, accusing it of interference in the internal affairs of Pakistan.

The US Ambassador to India, Dr Kenneth B Keating stated on 15 April in Bombay, "The phrase 'internal affair' is overdone and this is certainly not a case of internal affairs. The events could be described as the internal affairs only to the limited extent in that they are happening in Pakistan."

Mr Chester Bowles, a former US Ambassador to India, asked his Government to convene a meeting of the UN Security Council immediately to consider the happenings in Bangladesh as a threat to peace in Asia. He also called for ending of the US aid to Pakistan with the exception of food and medical supplies.

While the world was assessing the Bangladesh situation with sympathy, thousands of uprooted men, women and children were swarming across the international borders into India. They carried almost nothing, not even clothes. Hundreds were sick and many seriously wounded and shocked. They brought tales of horror unknown in history. This left a deep and lasting impression on the minds of the Indian population, particularly the Bengalis in India. The age old Indian tradition of providing succour to harassed and forcibly dispossessed community asserted itself and the Indian opinion crystallized under the shock.

Indian Reaction

The Times of India, in its editorial of 2 March 1971 said, "the last moment postponement of the National Assembly session gave Mr Bhutto a veto over the constitution making process. It is a surrender not so much to Mr Bhutto's threat and blackmail as to the pressure of the military bureaucratic machine in West Pakistan which sees in Sheikh Mujeebur Rehman's sixpoint programme a threat to its dominance."

On 16 March 1971, *The Times of India,* in an editorial 'On the Brink of Disaster', wrote: "But the international community as a whole owes it to itself to spare no effort to see to it that the innocent people of East Bengal, who are asking for nothing more than the right to manage their own affairs, are not slaughtered by the West Pakistan Military machine. The responsibility of the two super powers is specially grave here.... The Sheikh is not a secessionist. He is, in fact, a moderate. He has done more than anyone else to avoid a confrontation between the troops and the people of East Bengal."

On 19 March, it wrote: "But the world has never seen a non-violent revolution of such sweep and power as the one in East Bengal today. The people are united behind the Sheikh. There is no case in history where all senior judges have refused to swear in a Military Governor and Civil servants have of their own accord carried out the directives of a revolutionary leader."

The *Hindustan Times*, on 27 March 1971 in an editorial captioned "The Unmaking of Pakistan', said: "India has never desired the break-up of Pakistan. But, it cannot be indifferent to the suppression of the other half of Bengal by Military might.

Writing in *The Motherland*, Mankekar said, "Pakistan, as we have known it, is no more. Pindi might as well write off its eastern wing. History will name Zulfikar Ali Bhutto and Yahya Khan as the disruptors of the twenty-three year old state."

Frank Moraes, writing an editorial in the *Indian Express* (9 April 1971) said. "By its brutal action in East Bengal, West Pakistan has not only ignited a fire, it has blown the two-nation theory on which Pakistan was founded sky high. ... It is not India that has destroyed the myth of theocracy on which Pakistan sought to build herself. By lighting the fuse in East Bengal under the feet of her own co-religionists, Pakistan has herself exploded that myth."

Shri N.G. Goray, Chairman. Praja Socialist Party, said (*The Times of India*, 27 March 1971), "A conflict of this nature would not only affect the fate of East Pakistan but would also open the floodgates of anarchy in the entire region, making it easy for foreign powers to fish in troubled waters."

Mr M.C. Chagla, MP and formerly External Affairs Minister, recommended immediate recognition of the Government of Bangladesh, saying that the legally and validly constituted Government of Bangladesh had a better title to legitimacy than Yahya Khan.

Shri Jayaprakash Narayan—the Sarvodaya leader—advocated immediate recognition of Bangladesh Government.

The Indian Parliament, under the dynamic leadership of Prime Minister Mrs Indira Gandhi, passed a historic resolution on 31 March 1971. It says:

> This House expresses its deep anguish and grave concern at the recent developments in East Bengal. A massive attack by armed forces despatched from West Pakistan has been unleashed against the entire people of East Bengal with a view to suppressing their urges and aspirations.

> Instead of respecting the will of the people so unmistakably expressed through the election in Pakistan in December 1970, the Government of Pakistan has chosen to flout the mandate of the people.
>
> The Government of Pakistan has not only refused to transfer power to legally elected representatives but has arbitrarily prevented the National Assembly from assuming its rightful and sovereign role. The people of East Bengal are being sought to be suppressed by the naked use of force, by bayonets, machine guns, tanks, artillery and aircraft.
>
> The Government and people of India have always desired and worked for peaceful, normal and fraternal relations with Pakistan. However, situated as India is and bound as the peoples of the sub-continent are by centuries old ties of history, culture and tradition, this House cannot remain indifferent to the macabre tragedy being enacted so close to our border. Throughout the length and breadth of our land, our people have condemned, in unmistakable terms, the atrocities now being perpetrated on an unprecedented scale upon an unarmed and innocent people.
>
> This House expresses its profound sympathy for and solidarity with the people of East Bengal in their struggle for a democratic way of life.
>
> Bearing in mind the permanent interests which India has in peace and committed as we are to uphold and defend human rights, this House demands immediate cessation of the use of force and the massacre of defenceless people.
>
> This House calls upon all peoples and Governments of the world to take urgent and constructive steps to prevail upon the Government of Pakistan to put an end immediately to the systematic decimation of people which amounts to genocide.
>
> This House records its profound conviction that the historic upsurge of the 75 million people of East Bengal will triumph. The House wishes to assure them that their struggle and sacrifices will receive the whole-hearted sympathy and support of the people of India.

Mrs Indira Gandhi rose to her full height. On 27 March 1971 she said in the Rajya Sabha:

> We have watched the happenings, the elections in Pakistan with admiration. It aroused the hope that it was the beginning of a new future for the whole country, a future which will make them more united and strong. But they have turned into a long dark path, a tragic path, bringing suffering to the entire people.

> It is not merely the suppression of movement but it is meeting an unarmed people with tanks ... we are fully alive to the situation and we shall keep constantly in touch with what is happening and what we need to do.

She undertook a world tour to explain personally to various Governments the repercussions of the Pak military repression in Bangladesh. Her advocacy in the cause of peace was powerful but selfish imperialist interests of some Governments were even more powerful. Humane considerations have no place under such circumstances. Threats came pouring in from sources least expected to react in this manner. The horizon appeared dark. Muslim nations throughout the world tried to ignore the tragedy; some under the false sense of sympathy for the disintegrating Islamic state and some appeared shocked but were unable to muster enough moral courage to speak out the truth for fear of injuring the sentiments of fanatics within their own borders. The world conscience in general and Muslim conscience in particular was on test and it failed. There were notable exceptions here and there in almost every country who bemoaned the sad plight of poor Bangladeshis in which they saw the demise of democratic traditions and inalienable human rights but they carried no weight.

China threw its revolutionary traditions to the winds in the interest of expediency. That country by fully supporting the Pak Military repression in Bangladesh and calling it an internal affair of Pakistan found itself stripped naked to the open gaze of millions throughout the world, who relied upon them to support the cause of *self-determination*. They had denied this right to their own ethnic minorities like the Mongols, the Tibetans and the Sinkiang people. Tibet, in particular, had invited their special wrath because they exposed the Chinese betrayal to the whole wide world. The Dalai Lama, with thousands of his followers, had sought refuge in India when he was not even allowed to function as a religious head of a community which spent all its time in contemplation and research of Buddhist literature. Tibet was literally devastated by Chinese hordes. Spiritually oriented nationality of Tibet had no riches to offer to the invading Chinese armies except ancient Buddhist literature, their temples and their idols—some of which were adorned in gold and precious stones. Temples were robbed and then desecrated. Idols were broken and precious stones and gold taken as loot and war booty.

Then came the military dominated party machine, which sought to draw a line between poverty and abject poverty. Since Tibetan society had no capitalists, the head Lamas of monastries were bracketed into this newly created class. The whole basis of communist philosophy being class struggle, if there were no classes they had to be created in order to justify "struggle", which is the revolutionary ideal. The Tibetan tribal society, used to dealing with the vagaries of nature at an altitude of over 14,000 feet where nothing but grass grows, had now to deal with the vagaries of alien whims and fancies.

Food was rationed so that the invading armies could be supplied locally and the poor inhabitants, for the first time in their history, faced conditions of man-made famine. The rations allotted for local consumption could not meet even half the need of the people. They could not understand why under a communist regime their rations had grown less. Before, the Chinese invasion people had their fill of rations and even common peasants had several years' stocks of foodgrains in their family barns. They could not understand why the Chinese should rule over them and ruthlessly suppress the freedom which Tibetans had enjoyed for centuries and which all tribal people cherish above even their livelihood.

Poverty multiplied. Serfdom was now no longer voluntary service to monasteries but forced labour for alien masters. There was genuine apprehension that the Dalai Lama would be imprisoned and done away with under some excuse or the other. Even the Panchan Lama, who had joined the Communist Camp, met with some peculiar fate later. Even his whereabouts were not known.

The Dalai Lama, whose person symbolizes the Government of Tibet, according to their age-old traditions and constitution, felt that he could no longer look after the welfare of his people under an alien communist dictatorship. With great difficulty he managed to escape to India—his spiritual home (the land of the Buddha) next door. The world news correspondents awaited breathlessly for the news of his safe arrival into India since the Chinese Army and Air Force were carrying out a relentless pursuit to capture this important fugitive. On his arrival in India, he gave a first-hand account of what was happening in Tibet. True to his Buddhist traditions, he spoke in an attitude of sweet reasonableness. He deliberately played down the overbearing and merciless attitude of the Chinese communist invaders. He even praised Mao Tse Tung and blamed only the over-zealous Chinese cadres operating in Tibet. For his human attitude he was branded a bandit by the Chinese Communist Government and insinuations made that Indian Government had a hand in abducting the Dalai Lama into India with the aid of American CIA and were detaining him here under duress.

This background is necessary in order to understand the Chinese reaction to events in Bangladesh. Pakistan was doing in Bangladesh what their Chinese friends were practising in Tibet—a genocide of an unacceptable racial group. The Pakistanis had gone a step further and reduced the Bengali racial majority into a minority by sheer force of arms. They had well understood the lesson that power flows through the barrel of the gun and all guns were in the hands of Punjabis who constituted the real Pakistan. Sindhis, Baluchis and Pathans had no voice. The setting in Bangladesh was almost exactly similar to that in Tibet.

Chinese communists by their endorsement of Yahya Khan's repression in Bangladesh, stood exposed to the public view as imperialist adventurers in a new garb and it will take them a long time to live it down.

CHAPTER 3

Freedom Fighters of Bangladesh

Sheikh Mujeebur Rehman had, by immense sacrifices, won a place in the hearts of all Bangladeshis. He was their uncrowned king and they had demonstrated their love for him in no uncertain terms. Firstly, by electing all his nominees to the National Assembly; secondly, by all the judges refusing to swear in the Military Governor nominated by the Martial Law President General Yahya Khan and, thirdly, by all civil servants in the administrative machinery, resolving to obey only *his* commands. They had, with one voice, proclaimed him "Bangabandhu" (the friend of Bengal).

Sheikh Sahib was arrested from his own house by the Army authorities who first of all fired machine-gun bursts into his living room. He roared from his bedroom in his inimitably powerful voice, asking the military men not to waste their ammunition but come up and arrest him since he was ready for this eventuality. Something must have misfired in the Pak plan here since the Pak soldiers gave every impression of having come to kill him, a declared traitor. They appeared to have been taken aback by his courage in coming out in the hail of bullets and could not help arresting him when he was unarmed and without any intent to flee or put armed resistance, the two courses which they expected him to take. Since he offered himself for arrest, they were confounded and had no excuse to kill a man of his importance outright. Sheikh Sahib had been advised by his lieutenants to escape and lead the revolt from some safe base outside Bangladesh. His love for his people, however, was so strong that he told them he would suffer along with his people and would not leave them in their greatest peril. Little did he know that he would be flown out to a jail in West Pakistan and would not even hear of what was happening to his countrymen.

The details of his arrest got known only after the war. At that time no one knew about his future or his whereabouts. Rumours said he was killed already. Youth were furious and full of revenge. Youth leaders like his nephew Sheikh Fazal-ul-Haq Moni, Tufail Ahmad, Shirazul

Alam, Abdul Razak, Rab and hundreds of other known and unknown leaders, made their way across the border and were looking for someone who could give them arms, so that they could carry out an armed revolt against the Pak Military forces and throw them out.

Bengal Rifles (Pak Army Units consisting of Bengali personnel) revolted and, in some cases, were alleged to have even killed their Punjabi Officers. Some of the men under Bengali leadership kept on fighting till their ammunition got exhausted and then crossed into India. A certain Major Zia styled himself as Chief of Liberation Army, and announced on Free Bengal Radio on 28 March 1971 the formation of a provisional Bangladesh Government. He specifically said that the Government would be guided by Bangabandhu Sheikh Mujeebur Rehman, who was directing the freedom struggle from his underground Headquarters at Chittagong. Later, Syed Nazrul Islam, Vice President of the Awami League, was named Vice President and acting President of this Government and Mr Tajuddin Ahmad, the Prime Minister. Mr Khondkar Mushtaq Ahmad, Mr Qamaruzzaman and Mr Mansur Ali were named Ministers. This provisional Government functioned from Mujeebnagar and consisted of some brilliant men who, though originally taken aback by the violent turn the events had taken, slowly adjusted themselves to the aspirations of the determined youth, who were itching for an armed conflict with their erstwhile oppressors. I later met Mr Tajuddin Ahmad, the proclaimed Prime Minister of the Bangladesh Provisional Government. I found him full of admiration for Sheikh Mujeebur Rehman.

He said to me even if the Sheikh told the religious people of Bangladesh that there was no God, people would believe him. He added that given the alternative between freedom and release of Mujeeb, the people would gladly accept Sheikh's release in preference to even their independence. I was deeply impressed by these statements of his. However, being a mature politician, he did not encourage the hot-headedness of the youth leaders and some of them, therefore, did not like him.

I met Syed Nazrul Islam on a number of occasions. He gave me the impression of being the staunchest friend of Sheikh Mujeebur Rehman. He was now the Acting President of the Provisional Government.

Although he was supposed to be the head of the Provisional Government, he was not in the limelight. Mr Tajuddin appeared to be in power and dealing with all problems. Syed Nazrul Islam's only son Ashraf was undergoing training in some camp and impressed me as a determined youngman (he was hardly 18) with intense patriotic fervour. He had no time to even visit his parents who had reconciled themselves to this singular sacrifice.

Mukti Bahini

Colonel M.A.G. Osmany was the provisional Chief of Staff of the Bangladesh Army and in that capacity, the Chief of all freedom fighters. He advised his Provisional Government about all arrangements for training as well as deployment of freedom fighters against the Pak Military authorities in Bangladesh. Later, when the Government of India decided to assist the freedom fighters in training, Col Osmany maintained constant liaison with Lt-General J.S. Aurora, GOC-in C, Eastern Command, and supervised the training camps. He maintained the dignity of his office and had a very alert and presentable Aide-de-camp—a Bengali Captain who had escaped from the Pak Army in West Pakistan and, after great hazards, had crossed over into India. He had volunteered to undergo training so that he could immediately join the ranks of the freedom fighters.

Colonel Osmany had made a favourable impression on Indian Military circles because of his high patriotic sense, his loyalty to Sheikh Mujeeb and correct attitude towards all and sundry. I met him in his sparsely furnished office over a cup of tea. His smart ADC, who had undergone some initial training with us, knew me and received me well. Colonel Osmany was all praise for the type of training we were imparting in unconventional warfare. I met him later in Dacca after liberation in a party hosted by Sheikh Mujeebur Rehman. Colonel Osmany was now the Army Chief in the process of reorganising the Bangladesh Army and awaiting arrival of more senior Bengali Officer repatriates from Pakistan.

Thousands of trained freedom fighters, which included the regular units like Bengal Rifles, were organized into companies and Battalions under the name of Mukti Bahini (Force for Freedom) and fought alongside the Indian Army, but under their own leadership. They fought well where their leadership was good. They took on targets close to the border and generally attacked them commando fashion, for which they were neither adequately trained nor equipped. They often suffered avoidable casualties.

Some attempts were made to send them deeper into the country but unfortunately they were sent in large batches of up to two hundred. Small villages could hardly feed such large numbers and Pakistan authorities could easily find out the arrival of such conspicuous batches. On their departure Pak Military authorities would play hell with the village which had provided them shelter. This made their visits unpopular and hence unfruitful. Higher command, however, kept on pushing them in, without bothering about the consequences. Military plans tend to be rigid in timings and execution. There is no initiative allowed at lower levels. The highest commander on the scene is supposed to be the repository of unassailable wisdom and he is allergic to advice by juniors even in the matter of techniques of unconventional warfare about which he may know next to nothing. Ultimate success by sledge hammer methods smothers even proper analysis and innumerable casualties are accepted by all concerned as the inevitable price one has to pay for success.

Thousands of youngmen had volunteered for training. There were no satisfactory arrangements to check the bonafides and aims of all the trainees. Training camps depended upon the Members of the National Assembly (MNAs) deputed by the Provisional Government of Bangladesh to certify the genuineness of each trainee. MNAs blindly certified lists brought to them by Bengali officers, some of whom had their own political plans for the future of Bangladesh. That is why some batches just disappeared into the interior along with their weapons and some others came back after caching their weapons and reported the loss of weapons due to enemy action. A fool-proof remedy was suggested to eradicate this evil but it was not acceptable to people whose high ranks conferred on them superior wisdom also.

Bangladesh is paying the penalty for this mistake. It would take them a long time to get rid of this problem since it is widespread and has high enough patronage.

Mujeeb Bahini

During the period of turmoil we came across a dedicated set of youth leaders whose names were well known in Bangladesh. They were Sheikh Fazal-ul-Haq Moni (a nephew of Sheikh Mujeeb), Tufail Ahmad, Shiraz and Abdul Razak. My first contact with them left me with an impression that they were the only leaders who could deliver the goods. They appeared highly motivated, determined to do or die and proved beyond doubt that their leadership was accepted amongst the freedom fighters within and without Bangladesh. Unfortunately, the Provisional Government was in no mood to accede them any such status. They wanted them to train and fight under Mukti Bahini leadership, while these youth leaders had strong objection to such a course. Because of their stauncher loyalties and closeness to Mujeeb (they had all suffered incarceration with Mujeeb from Pak Military authorities), they preferred to be named as "Mujeeb Bahini". They selected and certified the genuineness of their own cadres who were their old colleagues. They selected and brought out for training from Bangladesh highly dedicated, tough and reliable men and insisted that they should have separate unconventional training as opposed to commando type training that the Mukti Bahini were getting. They appeared to head a political organisation which had cells in every important town, tehsil and thana. They were not certain about the bonafides of thousands of young freedom fighters who were getting trained by the Army and had never worked with them in the youth wing of the Awami League. They were, therefore, chary of disclosing their organisation or secret cells to them.

Colonel Osmany insisted on unity of command which, of course, in any war, is a most desirable factor. Some senior Awami League leaders who formed the Provisional Government were also not happy with the Youth Wing of the Awami League organised by these leaders, running a separate show. On this issue, there was no compromise on either side. The Indian Army accepted only the opinion of the Provisional Government, through its Prime Minister Mr Tajuddin and were not prepared to recognise any other authority, however effective and patriotic.

I could clearly appreciate the importance, a well organised and established, dedicated and highly motivated youth group has under such circumstances. I also understood the reasons such a group has for maintaining secrecy in circumstances where anyone could don on the uniform of a freedom fighter, get training and march off with a weapon into Bangladesh. Common sense dictated that we support Mujeeb Bahini and do our best to smoothen its relations with the more numerous Mukti Bahini which had won recognition with the Indian Army being under their direct command and of Mr Tajuddin who was treated as the Chief of the Povisional Government of Bangladesh by all concerned.

Mr R.N. Kao, Secretary in the Cabinet Secretariat, who was my civilian superior at this time, had the benefit of having detailed intelligence about the organisation of the youth wing of Awami League as well as its leadership, and was equally convinced that the youth leaders he had entrusted to my care were the only ones who could deliver the goods and needed a special status to allow them to function in the most sensitive political field in Bangladesh. He knew of the jealousies, which the ministers in their Provisional Government harboured against these youth leaders, because of the latter's hot-headed and uncompromising attitudes and their own (Ministers) ambitions and designs. He did his best to ease the situation wherever he could but mostly the brunt of criticism had to be borne by me, since I was the commander responsible for training and launching them.

My difficulties in this regard grew as the Minister in charge, Mr D.P. Dhar started going into the day-to-day details of our working.

A few words about the characters involved would not be out of place.

Sheikh Fazal-ul-Haq Moni

A sparsely built fire brand of man, who appeared to be their natural leader. He was highly dedicated to the cause of Bangladesh freedom and was prepared for any sacrifice. He never stopped working when he was ill which was often and I had the difficult task of sending a doctor to his hide-outs close to the border, and to get him treated as best as I could.

He was sincere and loyal to his friends and utterly devoted to Sheikh Mujeeb. I remember the day when I gave him the news which I had heard from one of my staff officers, of the Sheikh's release immediately after cease-fire. He cried in sheer delight and embraced me in gratitude. Unfortunately it turned out to be merely a rumour at that time.

Indomitable in courage and with high determination, he accompanied me during the actual war, through the most difficult terrain of Chittagong Hill Tracts. He was so careless about his own safety that I detailed a jeep load of escorting men, to see him safely through snipers bullets, when he travelled at night soon after the fall of Rangamati.

A man of high culture and few words, his laughter came straight from the heart and was contageous. I liked to see him laughing.

He was politically awake and deliberative, a master mind who easily saw through the game of others. A journalist of repute I thought he would make a good information and Broadcasting Minister of Bangladesh, though his ambitions appeared to be much higher.

He told me that I had filled the gap for these youth leaders in the absence of Sheikh Mujeeb. I knew he was merely showing his love and gratitude for what I was doing beyond the call of my duty for his country.

I later saw him after liberation edit *Banglar Bani*, a Bengali daily from Dacca, besides some other papers. He was so absorbed in this work that he had little time for me and after I made repeated attempts to contact him he would appear once in a while to say hallo.

Tufail and Razak respected him and so did Shiraz but only to a limited extent. Often the discussion would be hot. Shiraz and showed a good example of collective leadership.

Shiraz

He held radical views and was uncompromising. He would fight like a tiger and work like a dedicated slave. He could go without food and sleep for many days at a time living just on tea. When he ate he ate well. Chicken and meat with rice were his favourites.

He compensated for sleepless nights by sleeping long during days of respite. He did not like making speeches and usually some persuation was needed to make him speak to the Mujeeb Bahini Boys, when he had a very good effect. He spoke as a man of action and a worker at grass-roots level. He shunned publicity and wanted to work in silence. A confirmed bachelor, his style of conversation with his friends was aggressive and sometimes sullen. But he was very respectful to me. I cannot forget the day, when at Dacca soon after liberation, he came to see me in the International Hotel. He had been very sick and with high temperature he insisted that he be carried to my room. Even in the lift, two young men were supporting him, since he could not squarely stand on his legs. When I chastised him for leaving his sick bed to see me, he answered, "how could I miss paying my respects to you, who has done so much for us and our country, when you are in Dacca after its liberation". He was a lovable person and dedication personified. My only fear was he would not be satisfied with the slow march of progress in the removal of poverty and may even recommend some harsh and unacceptable measures and thus fall out of grace. As it turned out he never accepted any post under the Sheikh and became the leader of the only opposition to the regime.

Tufail Ahmad

He was the student leader who was responsible for raising hell to get Sheikh Mujeeb released from imprisonment on fake charges during Ayub's regime. His name was the byword amongst Bangladesh students. Whenever he appeared outside Mukti Bahini Training Camps, students left their training, forgot all discipline and ran to see their beloved leader. He was also highly devoted to Sheikh Mujeeb and adored him. Darkish and stocky, he kept the audiences spell bound when he spoke. He spoke with such fervour and force that his whole body would tremble and his face would sweat. He was tactful and pleasant even towards his opponents and was a politician in the making. He had a charisma born of sincere and hard political work which he had been doing as Lieutenant of Sheikh Mujeeb. I later learnt that Sheikh loved him equally and he was as frequent a visitor to Sheikh's house as Moni who was a near relation. Tufail worked day and night for the cause of Bangladesh liberation. His wife and other close relations were still in

Bangladesh and when I suggested a plan to get them out, he said. "Let us leave their safety in God's hands, there are millions of Bengalis in similar predicament. All cannot come out".

I was charmed by this man's natural friendliness. He repeated what Moni had told me that I was filling the gap created by the Sheikh's absence from their midst in these difficult days of struggle.

He was the first person to embrace the Sheikh when he landed in Dacca after his release from Pakistan prison. Even the sons came after him. Not unnaturally therefore, he became the Political Secretary to the Prime Minister in the new Government.

Abdul Razak

A well-built, stolid man who did not show his political incarceration on his face. Pleasant, cultured, politically mature and a good speaker. Organisational work was his forte. He excelled in this. He had led a volunteer Youth Organisation of Awami League and was extremely popular. Punctual and methodical, he led a well-disciplined life. He was industrious and prepared to make all the sacrifices needed to achieve his aims. I thought he would be the Sheikh's greatest asset as an honest and efficient administrator.

In that fiery foursome of leadership, he was the stablest character, not that the others were not stable but he always appeared like a granite rock around and on which solid structures can be built. He was deliberate and not too emotional. He had discrimination and thought deep and long on any plan before executing it. He would go into details and aim for perfection. Cinema going was perhaps his only weakness and he narrated with relish, how once Ayub's police caught him unwares, from a cinema house in Dacca when he was working underground.

I liked his sincerity and we became good friends. I thought Sheikh Sahib would use him after liberation for some organisational work and sure enough he got appointed as the Organising Secretary of the prestigious Awami League party.

It was a pleasant surprise to meet him in Delhi with his wife after their independence. He was on his way to Iran for a conference. He was just the same. He would be always an asset to the power structure of Bangladesh.

All these four leaders had broken out of Bangladesh and were looking for some one who could give them some armed assistance to liberate their country. No one knew them in India. Their own Provisional Government were in the process of forming and were not prepared to give them undue importance.

We were on the look out for some responsible youth leaders who had some hold in that country and after talks lasting several days we felt that they were genuine patriots, had a well established youth organisation with branches in each village in Bangladesh and would be able to deliver the goods. They soon collected the young men whom they knew well from within and without Bangladesh and we started imparting training to them in our specially organised training centres for guerilla warfare. Our training was tough but the treatment of instructors (who were specially briefed by me) towards these trainees was so good that a bond of friendship and mutual respect grew very fast between them. We noticed tremendous zeal and enthusiasm amongst these boys who were hand-picked by these leaders. All of them were educated and many had left their degree, engineering and medical courses unfinished in their universities. Some were mere school boys. Their ability to pick up instructions was fantastic. Boys who had never seen a rifle were handling light machine guns as if they knew all about them from birth. Wireless telegraphy techniques were learnt by them in record time.

Initially their physique was poor and they felt the cold winds in hilly areas. But they soon picked up with excellent food and vitamins that we provided. Every one gained in weight before leaving the training centre.

Those of them, however, who had left some near and dear ones behind with Yahya's jailors were sad and would sometimes cry bringing tears into many more eyes. Some narrated deeds which they had seen with their own eyes and that would steel the resolve of other listeners not to rest till the last Pakistani had been thrown out and possibly taught a lesson.

There were two teenagers amongst them, Ashraf and Jamal, who made tremendous impact on me since I was able to see them under the worst of circumstances and later the best when I assessed their future potential.

Ashraf

There was one Ashraf—the son of Syed Nazrul Islam—the acting President of Bangladesh Provisional Government. This young lad was the only son of his parents and was so highly dedicated to the cause of freedom that he spent all his time in the jungle along the borders of Bangladesh. After training, he wanted to utilise whatever he had learnt by putting it into practice. A handsome and promising young man who felt duty towards his country was of paramount importance. He also felt that youth must make sacrifices for they had to mould their own future. He was politically mature and resolute. He never visited his dear parents even once. I was talking to the President when a request came to me from Begum Nazrul Islam to ask her son Ashraf who had not seen her or written to her for months to come to meet her just once. I conveyed the message but the young man could never spare any time for his mother and never came till after the war was over. Syed Nazrul Islam was a tower of strength to the Provisional Government. He was unrelenting in his utter loyalty to the people and Sheikh Mujeeb. An unwavering and steady mind who although in the background, since Mr Tajuddin being the Prime Minister held all negotiations, lent dignity to the whole Government. His steadfast loyalty to his country and Sheikh Mujeeb impressed me greatly and endeared him to me.

Sheikh Jamal

The second teenager so impressed me that I started treating him as my own son and did not wish to part with him. He was Sheikh Jamal—the younger son of Sheikh Mujeebur Rehman.

This young lad had not yet done senior Cambridge or matriculation, since he was arrested along with Begum Mujeeb and the rest of the family and kept in confinement in their house from where all furniture was removed which forced them to sleep on the floor. The Pakistan authorities had erected barbed wire fencing around the house and put army guards around it so that no one could escape. No one could guess what was the plan of these Pakistani oppressors.

Jamal made a plan to escape and see if he could inform the Mukti Bahini the whereabouts of the Mujeeb family as also to see if he could fight for the country. He became friendly with a Pathan guard and jumped out of this wired prison. The going was extremely difficult and danger of Pakistan patrols lurked everywhere. Nothing daunted him; he escaped and joined some other students, who were making their way to India. He was spotted much later and taken in hand by our youth leaders.

I sent in a word that special care should be taken of this tiger's cub. Not only because he was the son of Sheikh Mujeeb but he had earned it by some of the most daring exploits in such young age. Jamal refused to accept any preferential treatment or food or clothing. He was really roughing it out and learning the art of guerilla warfare very fast. He went up in my esteem enormously when he told me that he had the reputation of his father to keep also. I knew then that he was trying to assume much higher responsibilities at a much younger age. He handled weapons excellently and enjoyed the cold climate of the hills. After training he moved to the border and shared the most serious hazards with his comrades. He worked day and night. When I used to look at his young innocent face, separated from his mother and family by a daring adventure, with fears about the very safety of his father who was imprisoned in Pakistan and with not much hope of early reunion, tears used to come to my eyes. I used to wonder how bitter he would become towards the Pakistanis along with his whole generation who were suffering for no fault of theirs.

Jamal was a born leader of men and so was his father. I used to watch his emotions when he heard his father's tape recorded voice in Bengali exhorting his countrymen to rise. Who would not be proud of such a father but he did not know whether he would even hear that voice again. I was told that sometimes he used to cry when no one was watching him. Not only for his father but more for his mother and his youngest brother Russel whom he had left behind under the care of Pak oppressors. He suffered in silence and became the darling of my whole family. We invited him to our orchard where he enjoyed and relaxed. My farm house had become the common halting place of all Bangladesh leaders. In one party in which Jamal participated I assured all assembled leaders that Sheikh Mujeeb will surely be released and ultimately assume charge as the father of the nation. I was speaking from my heart. Sheikh Mujeeb though unknown to me had become very dear to me personally and my family, and I prayed for his safe return.

After liberation, Jamal immediately rejoined his noble mother, Begum Mujeeb, at Dacca. Few people write about the role that these dedicated wives of renowed leaders play in such liberation struggles. I think Begum Mujeeb excelled all men in self-sacrifice. Living under confinement of the Pak Army on sparse rations, with not even a simple bed provided, would break any woman of lesser resolution. She suffered most and that nation owes a great deal to her steadfastness, her moral strength and character, and her unflinching determination in the face of heavy odds. This is what broke the will of Pakistani soldiers ultimately.

I met Begum Mujeeb soon after she was rescued by an Indian Army Officer, at some risk, after the fall of Dacca. Moni, Tufail and Razak accompanied me. I saw she had the grace of a queen and the ferociousness of a tigress. She exuded confidence, but was not certain if Bhutto would release her husband. When I told her that a Bengali Saint Baba Sita Ram Dass Onkarnath had predicted safe arrival soon of Sheikh Sahib, in the presence of her relative Sheikh Fazal-ul-Haq Moni she was somewhat satisfied. It turned out to be true. I had the good fortune to meet the whole family after liberation where even the youngest child Russel could claim having suffered for the cause.

There are two other instances where the sequel was not so fortunate. One young boy was so overwhelmed with emotion that he with a grenade in hand roamed the streets of an important occupied town in Bangladesh, challenging the authorities in broad daylight, to come and arrest him. Unfortunately in excitement he threw the grenade at a police party without pulling the safety pin out and it did not burst. He was tortured to death—a martyr.

The second is the story of unbearable tortures to which a young handsome boy trained by us was subjected. He, however, did not give out any information. Soon after the fall of Dacca Sheikh Fazal-ul-Haq Moni asked me if I could carry a Mujeeb Bahini sick boy in my helicopter to Dacca from Chittagong. I readily agreed. At Chittagong airfield I saw a group including ladies advancing towards my helicopter.

This young boy who could not walk was in the centre of this group and was supported by two friends. When he approached near he bent down to touch my feet a common form of salutation amongst cultured Bengalis, to show respect to their elders. I recognised and embraced him.

I was told that he was severely tortured so that he would divulge some secrets. Since he never spoke a word they paralysed his legs with electric shocks and beating.

I asked him whether it was the water from River Ganga or Brahmaputra which had made him so brave he said, "Sir, it was you who inspired me". Such was the magnanimity of those brave young men.

These self-sacrificing young men and women were the guarantees of ultimate success, whatever the cost.

CHAPTER 4

Political Wrangling

The 'Inseparable Foursome' was the name I had given to the four Mujeeb-Bahini leaders, viz., Sheikh Fazal-ul-Haq Moni, Shiraz Alam, Tufail Ahmad and Abdul Razak. They respected each other. They ate, slept and confabulated together. If, any one of them gave a pep talk to the Mujeeb Bahini Boys, he invariably mentioned the other three leaders. Amongst themselves I felt they accepted the leadership of Moni, possibly because of his relationship with Sheikh Mujeeb. When we were convinced that this leadership was responsible for the student revolt which ousted President Ayub from authority and had some evidence that they had the confidence of Sheikh Mujeeb we decided to give them all the help they could absorb. They were keen on training their boys in Guerilla warfare, the best expertise for which was with us.

Army could only train people for regular and commando type operations for which thousands of youth were coming forward and were being trained to form a force called 'Mukti Bahini' (force for freedom). These leaders informed us that many undesirable elements—counterparts of Naxalites in Bangladesh were getting training and weapons. They warned that these weapons would not be used against Pakistan but would be cached within Bangladesh, for post-Independence use, to usher in a sort of Naxalite rule. In fact they reported the names of known pro Chinese communist leaders who happened to be related to some Bangladesh Army Officers now in Mukti Bahini, with whose help and concurrence they were getting large number of communist cadres of their brand recruited, trained and equipped.

These matters were faithfully brought to the notice of the authorities concerned but apparently without any effect. There was another brand of freedom fighters in Mukti Bahini who was communal and pro-Pakistani. He was also determined not to hand over his weapons to the Bangladesh authorities after liberation, but to create chaos in the country so that Pakistan could stage a come-back. Fortunately, their number at this time was not large, due to the atrocities committed by Pak troops against all and sundry. There was a third type—a free-lance bad character or a dacoit who found this a golden opportunity not only to get most modern arms but to get properly trained at Indian expense.

I had clearly warned the Government that these three elements of Mukti Bahini mentioned above, would join hands, use cached arms and create chaos in Bangladesh after liberation.

In consultation with Mujeeb Bahini leaders I suggested fool-proof techniques of screening all freedom fighters which was not given effect to. Day in, day out these leaders would come to me and complain about this danger to their ultimate stability, bringing in fresh evidence. Equally regularly I would assure them that I would do my best to stop this. But I knew all the time, it was not possible in the circumstances in which we found ourselves. There was progressively increasing pressure to train freedom fighters of Mukti Bahini in large number. The emphasis was on numbers and they were available in the desired quantity. There was a perfunctory system wherein two Bengali members of the erstwhile Pakistan National Assembly were nominated to attest their bonafides. Every list brought to them by interested parties was attested without even a cursory check by these dignitaries of Awami League party. Once having signed the list they were not prepared to admit they had made mistakes in attesting the wrong people. The whole process was so casual that it gave the impression that either these MNAs were planted by interested parties or they did not care what happened to their country after liberation.

The Provisional Government of Bangladesh which essentially meant the Prime Minister Mr Tajuddin somehow did not see eye to eye with Mujeeb Bahini leaders and treated every one of their complaints as frivolous. Colonel Osmany took his orders from his own Government and though outwardly friendly to these leaders, did not relish the idea of their running a separate Bahini called Mujeeb Bahini, which was not under his overall command. General Aurora of the Eastern Command who was ultimately responsible for coordinating the whole operation was also unhappy since Mujeeb Bahini was not put directly under his command, this despite the fact that I had assured him as a soldier in command of Mujeeb Bahini, that the Bahini would carry out all the tasks given by him for execution, within Bangladesh territory; and that I would remain in constant touch with General Aurora to keep him posted with the results. He was not satisfied, since I myself was not being put under his direct command. General Aurora failed to understand the reasons for this peculiar command structure in spite of my best efforts at explanation.

The Roots of Trouble

Youth leaders always complainted that General Aurora had some political understanding with Mr Tajuddin, due to which both of them insisted on the Mujeeb Bahini working under their command and not under the command of these youth leaders who owed no loyalties to Mr Tajuddin. I knew that these youth leaders somehow did not see eye to eye with Mr Tajuddin who appeared to be conducting Bangladesh Government affairs with some elan. They were always respectful to their acting President, Syed Nazrul Islam but not to Mr Tajuddin.

I tried my best to remove the misunderstanding but it had its roots in the past and nothing could be done to remove old impressions.

The youth leaders somehow could sway the assembly of old MNAs and MPAs and did some adverse propaganda against Mr Tajuddin, usurping the role of Prime Minister when according to them it should have rightfully gone to some one else. I think that they had Syed Nazrul Islam in mind. This could have taken an ugly turn since the youth leaders were bent upon showing Mr Tajuddin his place as they called it. A split in the Provisional Government at that stage would have spelt disaster for the whole movement. I think I was able to convince these leaders that it was a move fraught with great danger towards the success of their mission, which was liberation of Bangladesh and would have even more serious consequences after the liberation. Fortunately, they agreed and although internally they grilled Mr Tajuddin, outwardly no one knew except a few friends like myself. I think Syed Nazrul Islam also advised caution to them and a grave political threat was thus averted.

There was yet another and perhaps a more sensitive problem which needed immediate attention. These youth leaders had actually seen some Indian officials confabulating with known Bangladesh Naxalites, in luxurious Indian hotels, where they appeared to be lodged. The youth leaders knew these men as their worst political enemies, during Martial Law days in East Pakistan. It was essentially against these people that the Awami League had started the youth wing. They could not understand, therefore, as to why the Indian Government should be giving their sworn enemies such preferential treatment. They therefore wrongly surmised that the aim of our Government was to establish a communist party on firm footing in Bangladesh, if not a communist government. They also learnt on good authority that weapons had been given to Marxists and Maulana Bhashani's men, who were being trained separately.

This was too much for them and as usual they came running to vent their spleen on me. This is how the dialogue went:

Youth Leaders—Sir, we did not expect that you would train and equip Naxalites and Marxists in order to nullify all that we have achieved in the last twenty-five years.

Completely taken aback and getting red in my face I said: What are you talking about?

Youth Leaders—You mean to say you do not know that Naxalites are being trained and equipped at ... (naming a place) and that Indian officials are lodging their leaders in top class Indian hotels and confabulating with them.

Myself—I have never heard such utter nonsense before. I always, thought some enemy agents would split us apart. Now who has spread this canard to you?

Youth Leaders—We have seen it with our own eyes and heard it with our own ears. There is no chance of a mistake in this. We are disheartened and wish to reconsider our whole attitude. We will never hide anything from you. We have always loved you for your sincerity towards our cause. It is possible because of your God-oriented nature, that your Government has not taken you into confidence with regard to this. It is entirely possible that they wish to co-operate with and please some foreign powers by this means. Kindly investigate and let us know your Government's policy. We can even understand pro-Russian communist party in our country, which in any case only exists on paper, being revived, but why the pro-Chinese communist party?

I was dumbstruck and had no answer. God alone knows I was not aware of any such move in our country. I myself had admiration for Russia who had done so much to support us in time of need, but I was certain no one in authority in my country, would help establish a pro-Chinese communist party in Bangladesh.

When I apprised Mr R.N. Kao about the view of the youth leaders, he surprised me with the revelation that Maulana Bhashani's Naxalites were indeed under training elsewhere. They had not been entrusted to my care, since he was sure I would not accept such a commitment and in any case my youth leaders would soon find them out and there would be serious trouble.

I was not prepared for this discovery. I have always had great regard for the Secretary Mr Kao whose competence and integrity were beyond question. He was also a God-oriented man and showed me unfailing courtesy and kindness. But here I had good reason to be annoyed. I faced an embarrassing position before these youth leaders. I was almost losing my credibility, through no fault of mine. If I had been told earlier I could have found some excuse to justify such a course of action or put it in a light that these men of action could understand.

Mr Kao simply said, "We have done nothing against the wish of the Bangladesh Provisional Government, who regard Bhashani's men as a great asset against Pakistan. How can we ignore their advice? Please tell your youth leaders that they would have to lump it even if they do not like it. We shall only support them as an important wing of the overall project but not as an independent political authority. Unless they behave we shall have nothing to do with them and they can go to hell" or words to that effect.

I knew he had spoken in a huff and did not mean what he said, for how could he hope to carry out his impending task within Bangladesh without the assistance of this most reliable and dedicated leadership which was his best find. Mr Kao had been working incessantly, under heavy strain, in a highly sensitive political situation with extraordinary success. I feel there were certain compulsions he could not possibly overcome. I was not convinced about the wisdom of this obviously wrong move to train unreliable elements and left his office much depressed in spirit.

I told the youth leaders that the authorities were naturally helping all those who in their view were prepared to fight for the liberation of Bangladesh on the recommendation of their own Provisional Government. That some undesirable elements may take advantage of this was entirely possible under these unusual circumstances and that they would have to remain doubly vigilant.

The misgivings amongst these youth leaders persisted. Therefore, they were all the more cautious about giving any information about their secret cells, safe houses or roads leading up to them to any one else except myself. I had given them my word of honour that I would not disclose whatever they told me of their organisation to any one else, unless they cleared it themselves first. This information was essential for me, since I did all the planning in cooperation with them. In course of our working together they had developed immense faith in me. I felt honoured and under no circumstances I would commit a breach of trust.

They would not divulge their secrets even to the important personalities within their own Government—their Prime Minister included. They strongly suspected Tajuddin of intrigue to oust Sheikh Mujeeb from power after Independence and usurp it himself. They candidly told me later "Tajuddin is in league with your communist Minister D.P. Dhar. We do not trust any one of them. Even your Government will not know what these two are planning for our post-Independence Bangladesh."

They would not give any information to Colonel Osmany who was working hand in glove with Mr Tajuddin or to Lt-General Aurora who according to their assessment was playing the game of their political opponents for reasons which they could not guess. They often told me that General Aurora was coaxing Tajuddin to meet Mrs Indira Gandhi and to insist on Mujeeb Bahini being put under his command.

Field Marshal FSHJ Manekshaw MC

The Eastern Command Headquarters had caused some misunderstanding between me and the Army Chief—General, later Field Marshal Manekshaw, who was my instructor twice during my Army career, once at Staff College, Quetta and another time at Senior Officers course at the Infantry School, Mhow. On both these courses which were attended by some of the brilliant colonels—who later became Major and Lt-Generals of the Indian Army—he had given me top positions and had congratulated me on my performance in both places.

The Field Marshal has one of the sharpest intellects I have come across and has a charm of his own. He is a brilliant tactician, very logical and broad-minded in his approach to any problem in life. He has an irrepressible sense of humour, which has created a lot of trouble for him in life. Late General BM Kaul had fallen out with him due to one such trivial incident. This was told to me by General Kaul himself. General Kaul had just built up considerable accommodation by self-help, in order to case the chronic housing shortage which was demoralising the Army. There had been a persistent state of emergency and the officers and jawans spent most of their time along the borders where naturally no family accommodation was available. After several years of separation from their families when they got posted to a so-called peace station like Ambala, they had to wait for their turn for accommodation which would take two to three years. By the time one's name came up for allotment of some measly accommodation, posting orders would arrive, for another spell on the borders. This was most demoralising. The matter was represented to the authorities concerned but chronic economic crisis never allowed enough funds for this purpose. It, therefore, occurred to General Kaul that something should be done with self-help. With his characteristic zeal, energy and influence in political circles, a project called 'Amar Project' was initiated and completed by him within record time at the lowest cost. Late Mr Krishna Menon who was then the Defence Minister, liked this idea immensely and so did Pandit Jawaharlal Nehru—the Prime Minister.

A similar project was sought to be initiated in Jammu where General Manekshaw was the General Officer Commanding (GOC). General

Manekshaw therefore, came to Ambala to consult General Kaul about this. During a dinner party in the Officers Mess at Ambala, in the presence of junior officers, General Manekshaw told General Kaul to swop commands with him saying "You are good at house-building and I am good at training. You take over my command in Jammu and construct houses while I shall train your division." All this was said in a lighter vein but General Kaul was a sensitive person and very proud of his ability in all fields. He did not take it lightly. This resulted in an irreparable rift between these two senior officers which had many untoward consequences later.

After the war the Field Marshal suffered again for some such remarks made in a lighter vein at Karachi, where he is reported to have told Pakistanis that they would have won the war, if he was their chief. This had some serious repercussions in political circles in Delhi.

However, when the history of the Indo-Pak war 1971 comes to be written, I have no doubt that the leadership qualities displayed by Field Marshal Manekshaw would occupy a prominent place therein. In any system where joint and smooth functioning of the three powerful, but independently commanded services, like the Army, Navy and Air Force is concerned, it needs not only an efficient but also a most tactful and charming army chief as coordinator. Otherwise nothing fruitful would be achieved. In my opinion the greatest contribution of the Field Marshal was to get the other two service chiefs to cooperate with him fully.

Fortunately for the country Air Marshal P.C. Lal and Admiral Nanda besides being brilliant in their own professions were also amiable personalities but without Sam Manekshaw things could have gone wrong a number of times.

The Field Marshal is handsome and smart even at the age of sixty. He is full of wit and charm. He would disarm even his opponents by being candid and fair. He is one of the few Field Marshals who would admit his own mistake and give credit where it is due. He is generous to a fault, a quality which under our circumstances does not pay in the long run. He takes you into complete confidence. He makes friends as easily as he makes enemies. In some ways he fits into the mould of those British Generals who must have influenced his long Army career.

He had a character which was typically English, like punctuality, proper dress, mess etiquette, treating trusted subordinates as equals and giving them full scope to air their views. This made him susceptible to be easily influenced by people who had easy access to him. To my mind this was a weakness which sometimes induced him to make wrong assessments of personalities.

His relations with Mr D.P. Dhar, who was the Minister responsible for Bangladesh operations were so close that I once saw him patting the Minister on the back. It shook me a bit since I could not visualise any service chief being that free with a Minister. Late Mr L.N. Mishra was also a great friend of his and they were quite free with each other.

I had established a good rapport with the Field Marshal but the Eastern Command Headquarters took every opportunity to queer the pitch.

I was subject to a dual control, the other one besides the Field Marshal's being political, during Bangladesh operations. The Field Marshal understood the whole situation extremely well and fitted my organisations—the Mujeeb Bahini and later the Special Frontier Force into his plans, so that he could derive maximum advantage out of this unconventional set up, without upsetting the special character of the participants.

Both Ministers Dhar and Mishra were very close to the Prime Minister Mrs Indira Gandhi. This ensured great political support for General Manekshaw who was rightly awarded the rank of Field Marshal after victory in Bangladesh. I think he had richly earned the rank. Under his military leadership we had for the first time in a thousand years of our history, won a victory of such magnitude that it changed the total balance of power not only in Asia but in the world and set into motion processes of peace which we had no right even to dream of. The whole world stood aghast. President Nixon of America made last minute attempts to change the course of history by posing an awesome threat of using their most powerful Seventh Fleet against us, though it made no difference to our resolution. We did not know at that time that the Soviet Fleet was shadowing it and Nixon could not take the risk of fighting Russia. By this magnificent gesture Russia won over the love of the Indian people. But I am going much ahead of the story.

CHAPTER 5

Mukti Bahini-Mujeeb Bahini

Naming Trouble

Mukti Bahini, organised and trained by the Army, was a formidable force which ran into several thousands. East Bengal Rifle battalions who had joined the revolt were already organised and trained. They were fitted into an overall plan. Mukti Bahini was manning all the Bangladesh borders in co-operation with the Indian Border Security Force, who had helped train them earlier. Besides manning the borders they were attacking Pak enemy positions close to their own bases along the borders. Their limited training, however, did not equip them sufficiently for commando raids against well prepared Pak positions and they often suffered severe casualties. But their own enthusiasm for action and relentless pressure of higher command kept up their tempo. Military command with little knowledge of Guerilla philosophy would send Mukti Bahini groups each consisting of about 200 members deep into Bangladesh territory and ask them to stay there as long as possible. The aim was to encourage the civil population to resist the enemy in all possible ways. Often this tactics achieved just the opposite results. Small village populations would find it hard to maintain two hundred additional men on meagre supplies which were insufficient even for the villagers themselves. Pak Martial Law Administrator always came to know of such large numbers visiting certain villages. After the Mukti Bahini detachments left, the Pak Army would come down heavily upon the villagers for having given shelter and food to Bahini boys. Several villagers would be shot as reprisals and the remainder felt frightened for the rest of their lives. This made Mukti Bahini itself unpopular in certain areas.

Those who protested against the fruitless waste of manpower would be subjected to the usual Army pressure techniques.

Some good ones amongst them fell out of grace and their otherwise commendable work went unrecognised. Lt-General Aurora who had the confidence of General Manekshaw rode roughshod over many a sensitive issue and our ultimate success threw into oblivion many a mistake which could have cost India dearly. His close contact with Mr Tajuddin and Mr D.P. Dhar also gave him great advantage.

The youth leaders had heard from their extensive organisation inside Bangladesh that some units of Mukti Bahini had acquired some bad habits. Some had looted and terrorised the public and others took revenge against personal enemies. As stated earlier all kinds of people had been recruited in the Mukti Bahini and although as a Force Mukti Bahini had done excellent work, some elements amongst them were reprehensible and gave a bad name to the whole Force. Youth leaders therefore, were of the firm view that their Force of selected Guerilla leaders, every one of whom was known to them personally, should be named "Mujeeb Bahini" to distinguish it from Mukti Bahini.

Their other argument was that the name 'Mujeeb Bahini was sacrosanct in Bangladesh and would bring them all assistance not only from their own organisation within but also from common people.

I think their superior loyalties to Sheikh Mujeeb were no less responsible for their choice of the name 'Mujeeb Bahini'.

We had trained about 10,000 Mujeeb Bahini leaders as instructors in various guerilla techniques and they in turn were supposed to train the whole of their organisation running into lakhs within Bangladesh. This was an established and dependable organisation with leaders who had worked initially with Sheikh Mujeebur Rehman and had his complete confidence as we learnt later. This meant that they had the confidence of the nation as a whole.

When I suggested 'Mujeeb Bahini' as the name of this special Force, it was not accepted by the higher command. According to them this would cause confusion within Bangladesh and possibly a rift between Mukti and Mujeeb Bahinis. I could not force a decision on youth leaders. They merely said, "Whatever anyone else says, these boys will be known as 'Mujeeb Bahini' within Bangladesh." This ended the argument as far as I was concerned but Army higher command was not prepared to accept a separate organisation, whatever its purpose. Not only the name but their entity was der question. Lt-General

Aurora said Mr Tajuddin was wanting to know who was raising this organisation and for what purpose? My explanation that this was a highly dedicated youth leadership to boost up the Awami League youth organisation within Bangladesh and to carry out Guerilla activity within that country, did not satisfy him. His heart was set on taking everything under his command and all arguments were therefore irrelevant. The Chief of the Army Staff, General Manekshaw, naturally went by his advice and on one occasion was very curt with me at Calcutta. I understand he was told by someone that I was deliberately using these youth leaders to raise an Army for my personal command. Several attempts were made by all concerned to talk to and pressurise these youth leaders into merging their identity with the Mukti Bahini or at least taking orders directly from the Army High Command and not through me. They refused point-blank and their determined and sullen attitude in response to such pressure must have stopped all further attempts in this direction. However, persistent pressure continued to be exerted on me since I was in service.

In a final bid to stop this controversy I met Lt-General Aurora to finalise the division of responsibility between Mukti Bahini and Mujeeb Bahini. He said that Mukti Bahini was responsible for all assaults within 20 miles of the border and that the depth area was the responsibility of Mujeeb Bahini. This is what the youth leaders wanted but he wanted them to function under his command to which they were not agreeable.

That other thing to be decided was the method of infiltration across the border which was held by Mukti Bahini along with the Army.

We had created wide corridors with safe houses throughout Bangladesh and Mujeeb Bahini boys had excellent contacts right up to the village level through their old youth organisation. They could come and go at will.

Lt-General Aurora insisted on knowing the point of entry at the border, the route being followed by my boys, their safe houses and their destination. Youth leaders had no difficulty in disclosing the point of entry along the border so that the Army units there could be alerted to allow infiltration. But they were not prepared to disclose their corridors, safe houses and destination since they suspected the bonafides of many Mukti Bahini leaders, who were their political enemies.

Army formations could not also be told this since Mukti Bahini was under their command and they were bound to disclose the whole thing to the Mukti Bahini.

With great difficulty a compromise solution that Mujeeb Bahini leaders only disclose the point of entry along the borders to the local Army unit commanders who would permit them to enter, was agreed to. All Army units were to be informed of this arrangement by the Command Headquarters. We waited for some weeks so that the Army units came to know of this arrangement and meanwhile established liaison with the local formation and unit commanders, through the Army officers of SFF who were appointed as Liaison Officers.

Lt-Colonels of the SFF were located along the borders to make liaison with the Indian Army easier. After I had received reports that liaison had been established but that the Army command had as yet issued no instructions to their units, I represented the matter again to the COAS, General Manekshaw. When the latter asked Lt-General Aurora as to whether orders had been issued by him and proper liaison established, he said that none of my officers had met any of his commanders and that he had already issued orders to all formations under his command, when I gave him the exact dates and timings of liaison visits by my officers, the Army Chief was quite a bit surprised and on asking Lt-General Aurora again, he got confirmation that my officers had met their commanders but that he had not been informed.

This was a minor incident and I would not have mentioned it but for our discovery later that deliberate attempts had been made by the Staff at Command Headquarters to misrepresent facts regarding Mujeeb Bahini to the COAS. As a result of this I had to meet the Army Chief several times to explain to him as well as his Director of Military Operation the true facts about Mujeeb Bahini. Major General K.K. Singh (later Lt-General and Army Commander) who was working as the Director of Military Operations (DMO) in Army HQ was a brilliant officer who understood the political implications of Mujeeb Bahini activity and their high potential quite well. He was a great help while he was there. Major General Gill took his chair after General K.K. Singh got posted to command an Armoured Div in war where he got highly decorated. The new DMO was a gallant paratrooper who did not take much time to adjust himself to his new office and except on one or two occasions we got on fairly well. He became quite friendly after the Force won its feathers in War.

General K.K. Singh had sent a very lucid note on behalf of the Army Chief to Lt-General Aurora about the command and control of Mujeeb Bahini and the tasks which ought to be entrusted to this Force. Despite this note there was constant wrangling and a lot of avoidable heart burning.

In any war, the Army commanders have to utilise the services of agencies which are not under their direct command, but do render full support under their own leadership, in the interest of common goals. All that is needed on the part of the Army Commander is to have a broad outlook and a charm which can get the best out of these non-Army men.

It would only be fair to say that during my discussions with him I found Lt-General Aurora quite reasonable except on this one issue of command and control of Mujeeb Bahini. General Jacob, his Chief of Staff, is a highly efficient person and a friend of mine. The genesis of all this trouble appeared to me to be political and these two officers cannot be blamed for this.

CHAPTER 6

Degradation of Pakistani Soldiers

In Bangladesh the atrocities committed by Pakistani soldiers after 25 March 1971 show a design which cannot be attributed to acts of individual sadism. They are too frequent and too many, and far too many people of the Pakistani Army were involved.

I have known officers and men of the Pakistani Army in pre-partition days. Their behaviour used to be upright and worthy of the profession. They came from religious and respectable land-owning families and they used to share respect for women folk along with their Hindu and Sikh colleagues. Some would have gladly given their lives to save the honour of an innocent woman of any community. Then what went wrong with the whole Pakistani Army, when stationed in the erstwhile East Pakistan (now called Bangladesh) for its defence and internal security? Surely a whole Force cannot run amuck whatever the provocation. Every officer and man cannot become trigger-happy at once and certainly raping girls in the presence of their close relatives, in broad daylight as a matter of drill, could not be for the sake of satisfying sex lust. Even brutes amongst men would not relish such beastliness.

There appears to be only one reason for the aberration in an otherwise well behaved force, and that is political indoctrination as well as compulsion. To this could be added the stupid fanaticism and selfish zeal of some senior Army officers to impress the political authority, in order to better their prospects in life. General Tikka Khan was selected by Yahya Khan to retrieve a political situation by terror, when his exhausted military brain could not think of anything better.

But General Yahya Khan could not have made the decision in a huff. Earlier he had told the whole of Pakistan that Sheikh Mujeeb was going to be the future Prime Minister. It was as a result of over whelming support that the Sheikh was able to muster during the first elections ever in that country, that Yahya had made this statement and had come to Dacca ostensibly to discuss the future set up of Pakistan with the Sheikh.

The plan was obviously hatched at the instance of the prominent political leaders who wanted a dominant voice in Pakistan. The master mind behind this whole nefarious plot was Mr Bhutto, the Chief of Pakistan Peoples Party, who had secured a good majority in the Western Wing of Pakistan, though not as significant as Sheikh Mujeeb's. Mr Bhutto's ambitions of becoming a dictator president of Pakistan was dashed to the ground, when the peoples' voice asserted itself as it would in any democratic set up.

It was Mr Z.A. Bhutto who advised reimposition of Martial Law and sending General Tikka Khan who had won great notoriety as a butcher of his Muslim brothers in Baluchistan. The need was for a fanatic soldier for whom the very words 'Islam in danger' were enough to smother any voice of conscience when engaged in gruesome butchery of innocent coreligionists, whose only crime was to ask to be treated as equals and not as second class citizens of a state, for which they had made more sacrifices than their rulers from the West Pakistan.

All available evidence shows a well conceived plot taken out of the books of Jenghiz Khan.

General Yahya Khan arrived in Dacca and gave the appearance of negotiating a fair political solution to the problem. He had prolonged discussions with Sheikh Mujeeb who, as expected, was adamant. General Tikka Khan had been sent earlier as Martial Law Administrator. No one in Bangladesh was prepared to administer the oath of office to him. This showed the extent to which the rebellion against the Martial Law Administration had spread.

Reports had reached Islamabad that political solution was out of question. Internal automony in East Pakistan with all powers except Defence and Foreign Affairs was the minimum demand of Sheikh Mujeeb and a communal dictatorship is least inclined to grant such favours. Mr Bhutto whose ambitions had been thwarted, went about fanning the communal flames still further, thereby gaining greater popularity in Punjab, the dominant military seat of power. The cry went up, "Kill all secessionists. Kill their leader Mujeeb. Teach them a lesson. Mujeeb is an Indian Agent." All Bengalis are Hindus. They are all an inferior race of intriguers. They need new blood—the royal

Punjabi blood to become true Muslims. Send General Tikka Khan there".

General Tikka Khan was briefed not only by General Yahya Khan but Mr Bhutto then riding the crest of a popularity wave as the new saviour of Islam. General Tikka in turn briefed his Army Senior Commanders and picked up a staff who would understand a Muslim Massacre by a Muslim Army. Hindu slaughter every one in that country understood but few understood why all Muslim intellectuals were to be killed in cold blood, why all young Bengali Muslim girls were to be raped, not to satisfy sex lust but as a religious duty to produce a new generation of blue-blooded true Muslims.

Lt-General Niazi could be relied upon as a determined Commander—well decorated, who would follow the policy of Civilian Massacre relentlessly and ultimately fight to the last man and last round, if the Indian Army came to the help of the victims.

Under the hoax of negotiations more and more shiploads of troops arrived from the Punjab and North West Frontier. Baluchis and Pathans of para-Military Forces were brought in large numbers, not only to let them loose amongst Bengali women but to give them a foretaste of what would be their fate if they continued to ask for their democratic rights.

When the Sheikh had finally turned down all sentimental arguments, pleading for still further sacrifices on the part of Bangladesh in the interest of 'Islam' (as understood in Punjab), Bhutto made his appearance in Dacca for no reasons at all. He had arrived to strengthen the shaky hands of Yahya Khan, the Martial Law Administrator, and to advise him what action to take with hell raisers like Mujeeb.

When all preparations had been made, General Tikka gave a demonstration of his clear understanding of his responsibilities by firing on unarmed labourers in Chittagong on 23 March 1971 just one day before General Yahya abruptly terminated all talks and left Dacca for Islamabad by Air. Hundreds were killed and their dead bodies were left to rot unburried in the open.

Before Bhutto left Dacca, he was so satisfied with this attitude of Tikka and his gang that he said, "Thank God! Pakistan has been saved".

I do hope some day the Bangladesh Government would publish an authentic and well documented report on the atrocities committed by the Pakistani Army in Bangladesh. It was an act of great statesmanship and extreme generosity on the part of Sheikh Mujeeb to agree to release not only the 93,000 Pakistani Prisoners of War but even the 93 criminals amongst them who had indulged in acts of beastliness, unheard of perhaps even in the ancient histories of barbaric people.

Only a sampling of what freedom fighters used to narrate as eye-witness accounts of atrocities is given here. The more painful sadistic accounts though verified by eye-witnesses have not been given, since the purpose is to bring out the causes of this tragedy and not to exasperate the feelings of Bangladeshis and other humans with a conscience.

The first major slaughter appears to have taken place on 23 March 1971, a day before the talks were ended and General Yahya flew back to Islamabad. On this day thousands of people started collecting near Chittagong port. Mostly they consisted of innocent village labourers. There was no Government order prohibiting assemblies. Without warning, automatic fire was opened up on them and soon the whole area was littered with dead bodies. The dead were later found to be over four thousand. Their bodies were thrown into the sea.

On 25 March 1971, the Pakistani forces entered Dacca University and went straight for Jagannath Hall which was a hostel for Hindu students. Over one hundred students were butchered mercilessly in their rooms.

Next morning Army units again arrived. They gathered all those who were wounded the previous day including Dr G.C. Dev, the head of the department of philosophy, Dacca University, and ordered them to collect all the dead bodies from different rooms and pile them up in the courtyard of the hall. It was a most difficult and painful task for bleeding and disabled persons but orders had to be complied with. After this painful task was over, all the wounded including Dr G.C. Dev were lined up close to the dead bodies and shot dead mercilessly. They were all Hindus and the Muslim God is supposed to reward the killers of Hindus.

On 25 March all the hutments of poor people, mostly Muslim rickshaw pullers of Babupara Basti near New Market, Dacca, were set ablaze with incendiary bombs. Machine-guns were already in position to mow down any one who tried to escape from being burnt alive. No one was to be spared. Children and women met their fate along with their men folk. Over one thousand were burnt in this inferno. They were all Muslims. There only fault was that they formed a part of a large mass of people who wanted to earn enough to be able to live their miserable lives.

On 26 March the same treatment was meted out to Muslims occupying huts along the railway line between Nilkhot and Hatkhola. Incendiary bombs and machine-guns took a heavy toll of people who had no chance even to see the butchers of the Army.

In Naya Bazar Basti, in old Dacca City, on the same day Muslim Awami League supporters were given the same treatment, but their young girls were removed to Army Camp for rape as a measure of mercy.

On the night of 25 March Pak Forces attacked East Bengal Rifles Headquarters in Chittagong. This formation consisted of loyal Bengalis who had served as a part of Pakistan Army for about 25 years. But they were not to be trusted any more since they were known to be sympathetic to Mujeeb's movement for autonomy. About a thousand men who were under training to serve Pakistan were lined up and machine-gunned.

Curfew was first clamped down on Sylhet town on 25th March about which none of the inhabitants were given any notice. An old man was coming out of the mosque after prayers when he was shot dead. The Army men then asked his two sons to remove the dead body. As soon as they came near the dead body they were both shot dead also. This pile of three bodies was allowed to rot in open view as a lesson for others who might venture out to the mosque for prayers.

Another instance is quoted of whole rows of praying Muslims in a mosque, being machine-gunned, with the remarks that they were not true Muslims and hence not entitled to pray in mosque.

Houses on both sides of roads and railways were systematically looted and then burnt. All women, even some old ones, were raped in the presence of their men folks who were later shot.

On 27 March a house to house search was conducted in Sylhet town from where most people had run away to the countryside. All women left in the town were raped including one who was 60 years old. After committing rape on one girl, they chopped off her breasts. The poor thing collapsed and died on the spot.

Collaborators, whether Biharis or Bengalis were not spared where the question of raping women was concerned. The daughter of one Muslim Leaguer of *Gahira* was taken away by the Pak soldiers after she had served them tea.

A Muslim engineer of *Zikatola* Mankeshwar who was working for Pakistanis was forcibly made to witness the rape of his mother, wife and sister-in-law in broad day light by the Pak soldiers.

On 31 March during day time Pahartoli locality of Chittagong town was attacked by the Pak Army in collaboration with Bihari refugees. About 3000 Bengalis were killed and all women raped. About 500 beautiful girls were dragged to the Cantonment and innumerable men used to rape them. One of these girls is reported to have remarked it is possible to stand the pangs of rape by so many beasts but impossible to bear the heat in body which results from excessive accumulation of semen.

Month of April 1971 was particularly reserved for insemination. On 10 April a village called *Nizirahat* in Police Station *Fatikchori,* Dist. Chittagong was cordoned off. No one was killed. No house was set on fire and no property looted. About 200 presentable women were raped by Pakistanis and their husbands and parents were compelled to witness these ghastly acts. They were all Muslims.

On 4th April in *Chhatak* the daughter of a Jamaat-e-Islami member, who was an enthusiastic collaborator of Pakistanis, was raped by four Pak soldiers in front of him and others.

About forty per cent population of Dinajpur district was of Hindus. Only a few could escape to India. The remainder were wiped out by the Pak Army. Some Hindus appealed to be converted into Islam and spared the agony of torture to death. None was excused. All were shot dead and buried in one pit. On the report of one Sital Sarkar that Hindus of Singia village about 8 miles North-East of Thakur Gaon were still hoisting Bangladesh Flag. The total Hindu population of that village consisting of about 1500 people was done to death in about half an hour and the dead bodies dumped in two large pits dug by the Hindus themselves.

Chittagong town perhaps suffered most. On 5/6 April the town was cordoned off, houses looted, women raped and after the rape naked women were marched to the River for a bath—all tied with ropes like cattle. About 50 girls were taken to Ramgarh military cantonment where each girl was raped daily by about 10 to 15 men. At the time of rape the Pakistanis would shout "Jai Bangla" the war cry of freedom fighters and ask their miserable victims to shout for help to their father, 'Sheikh Mujeeb'. Here all those affected were upper and middle class Muslims.

On 26 April Biharis (non-Bengalis) observed what they called a 'Revenge Day' in Dacca with the full cooperation of the Pak Army.

The area chosen in Dacca lay between *Mirpur* and *Samoli*, since it was mainly occupied by upper and middle class Muslim government servants.

The whole locality was cordoned off by Pak forces. Non-Bengalis were then let loose to satisfy all their sadist tendencies. After loot and butchery they raped every woman.

Killing continued while raping was being done. About 3000 Bengalis lost their lives. No one knows the number of women who lost their honour besides their lives. Those were some of the reason for Biharis being denied Bangladesh citizenship.

There was yet another cruelty practised which has no precedence in history. During curfew hours Pak soldiers used to collect all the young boys they could find in the houses. They were blindfolded and handcuffed and taken to hospitals where their total blood used to be drained off. After which their dead bodies were thrown in the river Buri Ganga. This is reported to have been practised at many places throughout Bangladesh. After all Bengali blood is not so bad for a dying Pak soldier in need of blood transfusion, and soon gets purified while it enters the blood stream of a Punjabi Muslim.

In the first week of May 1971 about 200 Pak soldiers attacked a village in the police station *Gazaria* on the border of Dacca and Comilla Districts. Hundreds of innocent villagers were killed without any provocation whatsoever, their properties looted and women raped. On completion of the mission the Pak soldiers were invited to dinner by the Muslim League chairman of Gazaria union, who had been helping them all along. The food was served among others by his own daughter. This daughter was forcibly taken away by the Company Commander to the military camp. No one till today knows the poor girl's fate.

Many talked of a most ghastly incident of torture of an innocent Muslim named Hafiz Mian. On 28th April at 7.30 a.m. Srimangal town of Sylhet district which had fallen earlier to Mukti Bahini, was bombed by Pak Air Force. As a result of heavy bombing many people got killed and the remainder fled in panic. On 29th April Pak forces reoccupied the town, looted property and raped women in their best tradition.

Now they arrested a certain Hafiz Mian who was incharge of one food godown in this police station and was stupid enough not to desert his place of duty. In fact the man was so proud of his loyalty that he did not allow any relative to run away since he expected some high reward from the Martial Law authorities when the town was recaptured.

But Hafiz Mian was suspected of helping Mukti Bahini to kill a Bihari Railway Station Master and allowing the local population to take away some food-stuff from his godown. No cognizance was taken of the fact that the other godowns had been looted and did not exist any longer. Hafiz Mian's godown was the only one still intact and still had stocks.

In the presence of the deceased Station Master's family, Hafiz Mian was ordered to be dismembered, bit by bit, while his own family members were tortured during intervals of these slow but most painful acts. First Hafiz Mian's fingers were chopped off and then slowly his arms and legs were cut off. While he groaned and shrieked in agony his family members were tortured one by one. This gruesome play took many hours. Three daughters of Hafiz Mian were raped and carried away never to be heard of again.

Then one Kuti Sen, a Hindu, who had not been able to run away to India, was caught and handed over to the Muslim leaguers gathered in the football field. A Pak Army officer gave a lecture which was explained to the Bengali Muslim leaguers by an interpreter. The gist of the lecture was that all Hindus were agents of India and, therefore, Muslims should kill them as an act of religious duty. Kuti Sen was tied with ropes, thrown on the ground and kicked to death by all present as an act of piety. Kuti Sen's son Babla Sen who had reached India on hearing of this incident came back stealthily and wanted to commit suicide when he saw the condition of the dead body of his father. Some people, however, persuaded him to wait for the day of reckoning which he did. He disposed off the dead body of his father. But some pieces of Hafiz Mian's dead body were still lying unclaimed even by jackals.

On recapture of Maulvi Bazar, Sylhet district, in the third week of April, the town was looted and all suspects killed. All fair looking young girls were taken to Army camp and raped. Next morning they were brought naked to the local playground and compelled to dance before the leaders of the Muslim League throughout the day. Then they were taken to Shivpur Army camp and nothing was heard of them again.

On 1st April 1971 a most horrifying thing happened in *Holati* village under Police Station Sobar of Dacca district.

The village was surrounded on all sides by Pak Army men accompanied by Biharis armed with daggers and spears. This was a pro-Awami League Hindu village. It was set on fire where even the cattle and domestic animals got burnt alive. Those who ran out were machine-gunned as usual except some girls who were saved for sadistic pleasures. Babies were snatched from their mothers and thrown up to fall on the pointed bayonets as an exercise in dexterity. The breasts of their mothers were chopped off and inserted into the mouths of the dead bodies. Those still alive were asked to shout Jai Pakistan'. Most of them did as they were told by the sadistic butchers. A boy aged six years, however, innocently said Jai Bangla' the slogan he was used to shouting. This enraged the Army men so much that they cut that boy into fifty pieces and gave one piece each to the Hindus still alive to eat. On their refusual they were all shot dead to the glory of Pakistan.

The few young girls who were spared the mercy of death were told not to be afraid. "We are not going to hurt you or kill you. You have been chosen to receive the good Muslim semen so that you give births to true Muslims and not the bastards like Mujeeb." These girls were dragged away to the Army camp at Tungi.

To exhibit yet another variety in their behaviour, the Pak Army men decided to treat the derailment of a train at *Goal Tek* on 27 April 1981 as an act of sabotage. Actually the railway track had given way due to erosion of the soft soil under the track. But Bengalis had to be taught a lesson and any excuse was good enough.

Four villages in the vicinity, i.e. *Goal Tek, Morkon, Pagar* and *Abdulapur* were charged with sheltering Mukti Bahini and committing sabotage. The villages were set on fire while the inhabitants were asked to gather along with their families in selected places in batches of about thirty. Here fathers and brothers were asked to rape their own daughters and sisters in front of the gathering. On refusal all of them were butchered including women and children. They were all Muslims. In some places people were forced to jump into the fire and were roasted alive.

There are too many instances to recount. They would fill the pages of history to the ignominy of Pak Army.

It must be noted that these cowards in military uniform who acted so arrogantly and fiendishly towards unarmed civilian men and women were shrieking to high heavens when they faced the brave Bengali patriots of Mukti and Mujeeb Bahinis, who were sworn to a manly and chivalrous conduct in war. Mujeeb Bahini—the elite of the freedom fighters set standards of soldierly behaviour befitting their name and role.

I had in all my talks during the training of the Mujeeb Bahini, insisted on a character worthy of such a revolution. I had said hundreds of times. "Every woman is either a mother, sister or daughter to you. Let even those belonging to the enemy look up to you for sympathy and protection. Every child is a potential citizen and helper. Even Razakars are to be converted to your way of thinking. Many of them are serving Pakistan merely to survive with their families, all other avenues of livelihood have been closed to them by the ruthless enemy.

Appreciate the Razakar's difficulties. How is he to get food except by serving Pakistan? Can you feed all Bengalis situated as they are today? If not, then do not antagonise a Razakar permanently by calling him an enemy agent. Let him keep his pride as a Bengali national by giving him some tasks which he can carry out easily whilst still in Pak pay."

In fact because of this training and action we had Razakar supporters throughout Bangladesh. They executed missions which could not have been carried out but for their patriotic help. I would not mention hundreds of instances in which our Mujeeb Bahini men and their stores as well as stores of the Army in later stages were carried by those brave Razakars who got paid by Pakistan and worked for their country's liberation.

The Character of Mujeeb Bahini was in sharp contrast to that of the Pak Army in Bangladesh. The Pakistani politicians were responsible for ruining the character of their excellent soldiers and will be answerable to these very soldiers one day.

But, any Army which allows itself to be used in a manner indicated above, digs its own grave. Soldiering is the noblest of professions. Killing of even the enemy is without rancour. Enemy wounded are treated at par with one's own in military hospitals and provided with the best medical attention. Prisoners and unarmed civilians are treated with respect. This attitude is reciprocal.

How can a soldier expect respect from people who loaths his very uniform. What chances has he of keeping his dispositions secret from the enemy when the whole population is seething with revenge. A soldier has to chose between woman and victory, greed and honour, selfishness and sacrifice. Any Army fed on the myth of its superiority over unarmed and helpless civilians, cannot face the truth of war. More than the Indian Army and the Mujeeb and Mukti Bahinis, the Pak Armed Forces were defeated by the ghosts of those they had tortured and killed.

The Pak Army of the East had lost its honour for all times since it had lost its soul and therefore, fell easily to the powerful onslaught of the forces of history.

CHAPTER 7

Involvement of Special Frontier Force (SFF)

It is not my purpose here to introduce mysticism into this account of the Bangladesh war, but something strange happened. I had gone with my wife to spend a few days with my spiritual preceptor 'Baba' Onkarnath—a Bengali Saint, at Banaras in December 1970. Baba hired two boats, one for kitchen and one for lodging and moved out to spend his time in seclusion on River Ganga. All disciples and admirers were dispersed, except about four who were in immediate attendance. Baba being eighty years old needed someone to look after his daily needs in seclusion (Agyatbaas). He was, however, kind enough to allow both my wife and myself to stay with him in this pleasant and Godly sojourn.

We spent four splendid days in constant companionship of Baba, listening to the sweet chant of Naam Sankirtan (Baba insists on musical rendering of God's name—Naam, in his presence all the 24 hours, by a special team of his singing disciples). Waves and small ripples on the waters of that holiest of rivers was music itself. One could hear the melody of temple bells from across the river morning and evening. One could witness the evening prayers (Aarti) with hundreds of lights being lighted on the river bank and scores of these lights left floating in the sacred river by devotees. The elevating presence of this God-saturated saint in the quietness of the deep waters of river Ganga at Banaras had an uplifting effect. I do not know till today why Baba did this unusual thing of making me live with him on the river-bed for four days and then just as I was beginning to forget the world to which I belonged, he announced the termination of our seclusion. This news was received by me with great dismay. I had never had such a pleasant time, nor had I ever felt so cleansed of wordly desires.

We returned to Banaras and immediately on crossing the river, Baba took us all on a round of Banaras temples. When we entered the temple of Durga (Shakti—or the Power aspect of God) I jocularly asked Baba to introduce me to this deity.

He held my hand and addressed the deity (that beautiful yet fierce image of Shakti) thus: "Ma, this is Sujan. He is soon going into war. Protect him and bring honour and victory to his Force and Bharat."

He then moved out of the temple, pulling me by the right hand behind him. On emerging from the temple I asked him what was this war to which he was sending me. At that time nothing special was happening in the world except in the two chronic war areas of Middle East and Vietnam and even there it did not look as if India would ever get involved and much less the Special Frontier Force.

In Bangladesh even Sheikh Mujeebur Rehman did not know what was in store for him or his country. The turning point of history in Pakistan affairs, 25 March 1971, was still far off. From all appearances it looked as though Sheikh Sahib would be accommodated along with his six-point demands of economic autonomy and possibly rule Pakistan as a great democratic statesman that he was reputed to be.

Baba gave no reply to my question and marched on towards his Banaras Ashram, enveloped in the sweet melody of divine music.

April 1971 brought refugees in staggering numbers from Bangladesh to our country but initially it appeared to be a problem of mutually satisfactory arrangement with Pakistan to feed them, reassure them and send them back to their own country. Sheikh Mujeeb was reported to be under arrest with Pakistan authorities although some including Bangladesh Free Radio announced he was directing a freedom struggle from within Bangladesh. Some said, he was dead and some within his Provisional Government acted as if he would never be allowed to return to his own country by Pakistan even if he was alive.

The tension grew from week to week and one saw super powers and some others with ambitions in that direction, doing all they could to intimidate India and boost up the morale of Pakistan.

Pak army was frantically preparing for a war in the East as well as the West and its Chinese ally continued to fan the flames of discord as well as carry out some proparatory movements of its troops in Tibet.

Under these circumstances no country situated as India was could fail to take precautionary measures against a sudden and unprovoked attack. After months of futile efforts by India's Prime Minister herself to persuade the nations of the world to help stop Pak massacre in Bangladesh, India was rewarded with Pak artillery fire, hitting right into the streets of Tripura, Cachar and Meghalaya states of India as well as villages along the borders of West Bengal.

Youth leaders were well aware of this design of their Pak rulers. From the beginning, therefore, they were preparing themselves for the showdown and even when their Provisional Government confabulated and dithered, they stood stout and upright determined to shed their last drop of blood for their only love—complete Independence. Within their provisional Government also, there were men of great status equally uncompromising on principles and drowning feeble voices still counselling restraint and reconciliation.

I Am Summoned

Suspecting it to be a long drawn-out affair, the Government of India sent for me as an expert in unconventional (Guerilla) warfare and asked me to study the situation by visiting the border areas and meeting people and to submit a report, which I did after a hurried visit to the affected border areas and meeting several Bangladesh youth leaders.

My personal visit confirmed what the map showed, that is Bangladesh was a paradise for Guerilla warfare. Forests and hills, rivers, streams and lakes made many areas inaccessible. Yet there was fish and fowl in abundance to keep a Guerilla Force functioning independently.

On top of that if you take on a disillusioned and angry population of 75 millions, one can visualise the Force needed by the martial law authority to maintain a semblance of order in any part of that country. Guerilla warfare I thought would suck Pakistan dry of troops and resources if it ever decided to retain this part under its possession.

Prolonged Guerilla warfare has some disadvantages as well. It is apt to demoralise the less determined civil population by not only enemy reprisals but natural scarcity conditions in such a situation. It also attracts foreign so-called experts on the enemy side, who treat this as a game of chess, to be fought from clubs and brothels, putting sufficient fuel in it to keep it simmering, so that they can retain their comforts and perks indefinitely. In course of time it can adversely affect the adjoining countries as well.

While still thinking of pros and cons I had the good fortune to be introduced to a darkish, wiry youngman in the house of a mutual friend. I think it was the month of May. This Bengali youth had been woken up from his well deserved sleep and entered the drawing room rubbing his eyes which had taken on a red hue rather significantly. We sipped tea together. He was charming, alert and sensitive. He replied to all my questions with the frankness of a simple school boy.

This was Tufail Ahmed. Ayub would have given anything to buy this young man. General Yahya on one occasion depended on this young man as his sole security guard in the country-side, where people almost worshipped this youth.

He talked hastily like an impatient collegiate but would soon calm down and smile that bewitching smile which came straight from his heart. He talked of his other three colleagues and soon two of them appeared. One was Abdul Razak, that Youth leader of Awami League party, and then Shirazul Alam, a fire brand who is sold to his country wholly—having no other ambitions. Sheikh Fazal-ul-Haq Moni met me much later. After meeting Moni I felt convinced that that foursome with complimentary qualities and unparalleled dedication could deliver the goods and could be entrusted with responsibilities.

These leaders frankly explained to me the infrastructure of dedicated political workers they had left behind in Bangladesh, who were brave, mature and highly respected. All they needed was proper Guerilla/Commando type training and suitable weapons. They also confined their opposition to some communist cadres at well as fanatic communalists who were preparing the ground for their patrons in China and Pakistan and with whom under no circumstances would they cooperate even if it meant delaying their independence for some more years and making more sacrifices.

They said these opponents of theirs in Bangladesh were opportunists and had no principles. They had some friends in Muzafar Group (pro-Russian Communists) but according to them the group had no following worth the name either amongst the labour or students. I later met Prof Muzafar at the instance of Mr DP Dhar and found him quite a dedicated person to his cause.

Incidently I might mention here that I met Maulana Bhashani of Bangladesh in Rishikesh in October 1971. He had come down in a very comfortable limousine to meet Baba Onkarnath, that great Bengali saint who has an Ashram at Rishikesh. Bhashani was well known in India as a Hindu hater, who was also reputed to be responsible for large Hindu killings during partition; it was quite a surprise therefore, when he landed along with a retinue of Government of India officers and his own secretaries. At 90 he appeared to be in the pink of health. With me he talked of the courage of Sikhs. He gave the impression that he loved India and expected Indian armed help for the liberation of his country.

Baba had also heard a lot about him but showed him courtesy and consideration. Maulana Bhashani asked Baba in Bengali if Bangladesh would be free, and how soon. Baba replied, "what you are asking for has already been ordained by God and would soon happen. It is only a question of turning the pages of history as intended by God for the future". Maulana Bhashani was very pleased with this reply and asked his secretary to write it down in the diary as a prediction of this great saint. Baba then took him on a round of the Ashram, explained all activities to him and ultimately ordered some fruits (Prasad—a gift by Saints) to be served to Maulana and his friends in Baba's own living room. This was a rare gesture of goodwill by Baba and I am sure that the Maulana appreciated this and went out showing considerable respect to Baba.

For quite some time Baba had been praying for the Independence of Bangladesh. Durga Pooja (worship of Shakti Deity) was going on as usual at this time in his *Rishikesh* Ashram. At the end of the Pooja the image is immersed in River Ganga. This time the image was given no farewell on the due date. Baba told everyone, "Ma is going to stay with me a little longer. We have to discuss certain things". He was noticed crying and talking to this image in this fashion. "Ma, I shall bid you farewell tonight by immersing you in River Ganga. Go straight with the waters of this river into Bangladesh. Thousands are crying there.

They are being tortured, humiliated and killed. Save them Ma. Throw out the brutes and free this God-oriented nation. They depend on you Ma, Sujan and some other desciples of mine will also be there fighting this war. Protect them. Bring honour and glory to their Arms oh destroyer of unrighteousness...."

He tearfully departed from this image that night and his closest associates knew where the war was going to be and with what results. I was told all this after the war.

By now I had already been entrusted with this politicomilitary task of training and organising this formidable Guerilla Force for Bangladesh which was to be recruited by the youth leaders. I was to plan the whole Guerilla operation in consultation with these leaders and carry out the plans under my personal supervision. I could not have asked for anything more soul satisfying. It took all my time. It was not a textbook situation. It was something unique and needed thorough and detailed study and my total energy.

While this was going on. I was thinking it might be a good opportunity to use the Special Frontier Force against fierce Pathan and Mizo para-military forces now deployed by Pakistan, in some of the most difficult jungle terrain of Chittagong Hill Tracts. These Pak para-military forces were supported by regular Pakistan Army brigades as well as Pak Air Force and were threatening our Army's most sensitive flank, besides securing the Arakan Road—the only land route of withdrawal open for Pak troops to escape into Burma if defeated by our Army.

Apparently General Manekshaw had been thinking on similar lines and one day sent for me to investigate this possibility. Our minds met and I set out to prepare this special Force of Northern Hill Tribes for this new venture. Leaders and men of this force did not take much time to understand the full implication of joining this venture and they made a representation in writing that they be allowed to participate and make some contribution if ever Pakistan forced this war on this country. This was gratefully accepted and now I had two Fighting Commands. SFF directly as a Commando Force and Mujeeb Bahini (the Guerilla Force) which was later also referred to as SAMS boys, named after General Sam Manekshaw, who told Mr Tajuddin Ahmad that he himself had organised this force to carry out special tasks for the Army. This ended the old controversy as to who raised them and for what purpose.

But let us first discuss the Mizos and the terrain both of which were capable of adversely affecting the situation.

CHAPTER 8

Mizos

This tribe inhabits the Lushai Hills which now constitute a separate state called *Mizoram* in India. They are of Mongoloid origin, and normally a docile and peace-loving people. Some of them live in the adjoining Chin Hills of Burma. Due to the scattered nature of their settlements, the British the overall ruling authority, put them under the administrative control of the then Governors of Assam, Bengal and Burma.

It is believed that an attempt was made in 1892 to see if all these areas could be united under one administrative control. But the British authority did not find it feasible. The State Act of India 1935 made about 16,000 square miles of Mizo territory in India the special responsibility of the Governor-General-in Council. The British Government banned any kind of political organisation in these sensitive border areas, but British missionaries were given full facilities to convert these simple tribes into Christians and spread Western education and culture into these areas as much as they could absorb. This was a part of a long term policy of the British to keep a foothold between India and Burma—both on the verge of Independence. The troubles of these simple and lovable people commence as a result of this policy.

In April 1946, the British Government lifted the ban on formation of political parties. At this time the *Mizo Union* party was organised. Mr Ch Saprawnga, the Vice-President of this party, was taken as a member of the Parliament from this part.

Another organisation called the United *Mizo* freedom organisation sent a delegation under its President Mr Lalmavia to meet U-NU, the Prime Minister of Burma, to work out their aim of integration with Burma. This was not encouraged by the Burmese authorities.

The third political party, *Mizo Union Council* advocated reunification for sovereignty. This was led by men who had been turned out from the more powerful *Mizo Union* which aimed at union with India.

At this point Mr Macdonald, the British Political Officer, played the notorious villain's role and wrote pamphlet after pamphlet to educate people in what he called their self-determination. He used the Church leaders and Missionaries to warn Mizos about their cultural and religious exploitation by India and the impending danger of their complete Indianisation and losing the recently acquired Western tastes. He went to the extent of threatening *Mizo Union* leaders with dire consequences if they did not stop towing the line of the Indian National Congress, the majority freedom party of India. He told them, "You would be treated as traitors and the future generation would dig your very bones out of the graves and scatter them in muck."

Mr Macdonald even drafted a Free Mizoram Constitution as a parliamentry democracy, having two houses—Upper and Lower—on the analogy of the British Parliament. He commandeered the support of Ex-Servicemen's Association and the Lushai Chiefs Council (both directly under the thumb of the Political Agent) and the Mizo Union Council party. But he failed in his attempt to take this essentially 'Macdonald proposal' directly to His Majesty's Government in London. This proposal had an essential flaw which antagonised the majority of Mizos. According to this proposal the village Chief, who exercised immense hereditary powers of dictators, were to retain their dominant position. Mizo Union party on the other hand told people that as part of Indian Republic, the Chieftainship would be abolished and common men would have a voice. Mizos Independent tribal character loved this slogan and Mizo Union party carried the day.

The nefarious activities of Mr Macdonald were taken up later by the British Superintendent of Lushai Hills Mr L.L. Peters. He hastily organised a political committee of the leaders of the following parties which existed mostly on paper, i.e. representatives of different churches, representatives of village chiefs council, Ex-Servicemen's Association and representatives of women welfare organisation. He himself became the chairman who drafted a resolution on behalf of all these people and presented it to the Governor of Assam.

In essence this Resolution asked the British authority to clarify whether Lushais (Mizos) were allowed to join any dominion of their choice like Burma or Pakistan or were they already recognized as a part of Indian union. The Resolution called upon the British authority to ensure that their customary laws and land tenure be safeguarded and that the Lushais be allowed to opt out of the Indian union whenever they wish to do so after ten years. This Resolution is dated 14 August 1947. His Excellency the British Governor of Assam did not reply to this communication, which shows that the British authority as such was not in favour of causing further unrest along these sensitive borders at that stage.

However, men like L.L. Peters and some missionaries continued and intensified their nefarious activities.

On 22 October 1961, a new political party was organised in *Mizoram* called the *Mizo National Front* (MNF). Mr Laldenga, the Founder President and Mr Lalnummavia, the Vice-President, were arrested in 1963 for visiting Pakistan without proper travelling documents and for the purpose of conspiring against India. They were however, released two months later because of the conciliatory policy of the Government of India.

A delegation of the MNF under its President Mr Laldenga met the Late Mr Lal Bahadur Shastri at Gauhati, Assam, on 30 October 1965. They expressed their desire to form an Independent Mizoram State and to make it economically viable, pressed for merger of adjoining territories with Mizo population in India, as well as in Chin Hills of Burma. The late Prime Minister gave them a patient hearing and said he would communicate with them later.

In spite of their officially declared non-violent approach towards the solution of this political problem Mr Laldenga and his party, organised Guerilla bands and in connivance with Pakistan authority made their bases in Chittagong Hill Tracts just across the Indian Borders.

From these secure bases and with the latest weapons and Guerilla training acquired under Chinese instructors, through the good offices of Pakistan, they carried out their depredations into the Indian territory of *Mizoram*.

These simple misguided tribals have failed to make a correct appreciation of the situation which confronts them. Their insignificant numbers, inhabiting a land-locked hilly terrain, with no communication

The author with the four leaders of the Guerilla Movement
From left to right: Shiraz, Sheikh Fazlul Haq Moni,
Tufail Ahmed and Abdul Razak

The author with the leaders of the Guerilla Movement

Two 'Tiger Cubs' under training for the liberation of Bangladesh with the author. Sheikh Mujib's son Jamal is on the left and Ashraf, the son of the Acting President, Syed Nazrul Islam is on the right.

The author with two youth leaders

The author with two great spiritual leaders,
Baba Onkarnath and the Dalai Lama

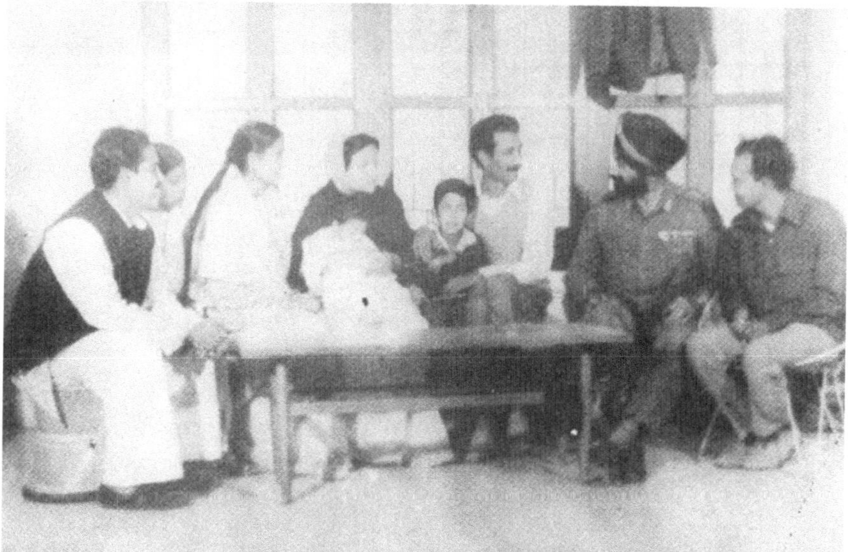

The author with Sheikh Mujib's family in their house

Gen. Uban being decorated with the Param Vishist Seva Medal by the late President V.V. Giri

The author being received by the local population after the capture of Rangamati

Evacuation of casualties by the Special Frontier Force. The terrain caused considerable difficulty in this task

The author addressing a large gathering somewhere in India

An improvised flotilla used for the attack on Rangamati

After the capture of Rangamati, the author seen here at the house of the Collector which was used as his office

SFF personnel being trained in paradropping

Training of SFF personnel. Photographs show improvised training aids that were used for ground practice for paratroopers

like roads and railways, no agricultural land or minerals and few forest products, signify no good economic or other prospects for their future. It is obviously in their interest to remain a part of the developing country like India and get their scarce resources developed by India.

As India's sentinals along their sensitive borders they have much to gain from India—the only country in this region which is in a position to assist *Mizoram* financially.

Taking the cause of *Mizo* discontent there is considerable substance in their anger against India. British authority did nothing for them except giving them false values of Western life and civilisation and the Missionaries tried to create a rift between this fine Christian Mizo community and the rest of the country, by denigrating Indian culture and religious thought. Indians did nothing better except treating them as a museum piece and highlight only their folk dances. Little effort has been made to remove their hunger by improving agriculture, or build up even small-scale industries for which *Mizos* can find good craftsmen. There is no machinery worth the name in the whole state. There are no roads except the main highway connecting Aizawal, the capital, with the rest of India. There is a great dearth of hospitals and schools. Frustration is writ large on the faces of these fine men and women and yet they manage to laugh off their miseries. God alone knows how.

By and large the simple tribes only want to earn their livelihood in peace. A good administration which has an understanding of their character and problems would revolutionise the situation in five years and establish the foundations of a society consisting of loyal and sturdy men who can be entrusted with the security of that border. What is required is administration with a missionary zeal, who respect the traditions and the new Christian religion of these fine people. Security forces are not meant to pacify people. At best they can irritate them by their arrogant behaviour. The security forces have to be briefed properly so that they do not treat every *Mizo* as hostile.

The discontent amongst *Mizos* was fairly widespread in Mizoram and their secure bases in Chittagong Hill Tracts were well stocked by Pakistan and China to oppose any likely Indian infiltration into this inhospitable land.

These Mizos were on the pay roll of Pakistan Para-Military Forces in Bangladesh who had been trained by the Chinese in Guerilla warfare and equipped and deployed by Pakistan in Chittagong Hill Tracts. They were working jointly with Pak Para-Military Forces. Pak authorities maintained small units of Baluchis, Pathans and Punjabis alongside Mizos in every post, to make sure they fought to the last man and last round in the interest of Pakistan. We shall discuss them further in subsequent chapters and bring out their fighting and other qualities.

Let us first study the terrain of our operation—the Chittagong Hill Tracts.

CHAPTER 9

Terrain of Chittagong Hill Tracts

It is a hilly terrain with thick forests. There are four distinct hill ranges interspersed with khals (rivulets) which get swollen to immense sizes if River Karnaphuli can be blocked and Kaptai Dam is the key to this.

River Karnaphuli cuts across the terrain from *Demagiri* (Indian outpost) in the North East to *Chittagong Port* in the South West. The river is navigable for the most parts and important towns of *Barkal, Subalong, Rangamati, Chandarghona* and *Chittagong* are all located along its course.

Kasalang Khal running North to South joins this river at *Subalong*. It also has several important towns along its course and is navigable. *Chingri Khal* running parallel to this joins river Karnaphuli at Rangamati. It also has some important habitations. There are hundreds of other khals and lakes.

River Karnaphuli and these two khals are the main arteries of communication and key to any military success in this extremely difficult terrain.

Foot tracks, where they exist, are along the crest of the hills. Snakes and other undesirable creatures abound in this area. Dysentery is common and so is malaria and many other tropical diseases.

River *Sangu* further South follows a course from South East to North West and is bridged for Arakan Road at *Do Hazari*, later a vital target for destruction assigned to SFF.

Eastern border of Chittagong Hill Tracts adjoins the *Mizoram* State of India with some border posts all maintained by air, except for Demagiri up to which a fair road runs from *Aizawal*. Across this border, Mizo rebels infiltrate in and out to their inaccessible but well stocked bases in Chittagong Hill Tracts, through the connivance of Pakistan authorities.

The Buddhist Chakma tribe that inhabits this area had no sympathies with the aspirations of Bangladeshis for Independence. In fact,

Mr Tridip Roy—their Raja—has tried to remain in touch with them from Islamabad to persuade them into an anti-Bangladesh posture.

Both Mizos and Chakmas were to play a highly inimical role during our operations.

It is only after my operational stay in these parts that I fully understood the significance of the British plan to establish a pro-West Christian Mizo land comprising all parts in Burma and Assam inhabited by Mizos. This same plan appears to have been persued by the Chinese in this area on an enlarged scale incorporating Nagaland as well. In enemy hands this could be a most formidable Guerilla base endangering the security of the whole of South Asia.

The plains of Chittagong also have considerable vegetation and only two roads running North to South.

Then there is the famous Arakan Road which is the only land link between Bangladesh and Burma and the only escape route for the trapped enemy in Dacca and Chittagong.

The terrain is also subject to typhoons of severe intensity. We experienced onc as we were concentrating for action. It blew the hut roofs, walls and trees. Only dug in positions are safe. Anything above ground is not.

Minds Meet

Army Chief Sam Manekshaw known as 'Sam' to his friends and admirers was bent upon using all available resources to win this war which, it appeared certain, Pakistan would launch. He had apparently made up his mind to use the Special Frontier Force in the most difficult terrain of Chittagong Hill Tracts, consisting of trackless jungles and hills surrounded on all sides by water.

Firstly, there was the famous Kaptai Dam producing power for East Pakistan which he wanted destroyed. Since it was located in the heart of this wild area, only Guerilla action could destroy it. Destruction of this structure would flood the whole of this area and make it a nightmare for Pakistan's Regular and Para-Military forces deployed there.

Secondly, there was the famous *Arakan Road* leading from Dacca to Chittagong and thence to Cox's Bazar and Burma along the Coast. This was the only land-route of withdrawal for Pak Army troops into Burma and safety. This was also the only route for use by the Pak Army in case the American Seventh Fleet came into the Bay of Bengal to retrieve the fleeing Pak Army. Some of the best beachhead areas being South of Chittagong Port, the importance of the security of this road for the Pak Army cannot be over-stressed.

Thirdly, the Chittagong Port itself was the main port at which all reinforcements of men and material were being landed from Pakistan as well as its allies. It was as vital for the Indian Army to threaten and close this port as it was for the Pak Army to defend it at all costs. It was their life line. In recognition of this fact the Pak authorities had deployed approximately 8000 men, Regular and Para-Military troops, in this area.

There was yet another reason which gave added importance to this area and that was that Chittagong Hill Tracts threatened the Eastern flank of the Indian Army Corps poised to strike towards Dacca. It was vital therefore to remove this threat.

General Manekshaw had, therefore, planned to use the tough Guerillas of SFF to dominate this area during the war, since this was the only force which could fight without Artillery and Air support and even for extensive water crossings which depend upon local improvisation. With his penetrative intellect he had hit upon the best solution to this problem.

Meanwhile I had also been thinking of a suitable area in which SFF could be used in the event of a war with Pakistan. I had a dual capacity. Having trained Mujeeb Bahini I was responsible for their deployment deep into Bangladesh territory and control the overall insurrection. This I could have done by moving to a suitable location close to the Bangladesh borders and remaining in touch with my sector commanders functioning along each border. But, I thought the best thing would be to penetrate deep into a secure area within Bangladesh from where to conduct this whole operation. And what could be a better area than the secluded Chittagong Hill Tracts? I also wanted to use this force in a somewhat independent role so that we and the Indian Army did not come in the way of each other. I have a natural apathy for fighting in a role where your tactics are dictated by an inflexible regular soldier who holds all the resources to support your action. Nothing could be less fruitful in war for a Guerilla Force. I was praying therefore, that if ever the call came for the SFF to take part in this war I should be allotted this difficult but congenial theatre of operations—the Chittagong Hill Tracts, where I could be more or less independent of the Army to give full scope to the initiatives of my men. To our great good fortune this is what ultimately happened.

The Army Chief sent for me and explained what he had in his mind about the role of Special Frontier Force in War. This was exactly as I had visualised. Our minds met and I was immediately told to get ready for the task. I came back quite happy and started preparing my plans for moving into the area of operations.

Our secret move was to be carried out with the help of air transportation up to a certain point. From there we were to be moved in Army vehicles to our road-head. At this point all men were to be assembled and sent forward on foot carrying their equipment on man-pack basis. It meant an intricate move plan which depended to a large extent on the goodwill and efficiency of other agencies and had to be worked to the last details. While this planning was going on I got the much awaited orders from Army Headquarters in the shape of "instruction" addressed to me.

Much Ado about Nothing

'Instruction' is a term used in the Army signifying an order to an independent commander which leaves almost total initiative in the hands of the recipient for the conduct of the operation. Instruction is a guideline and has to be implemented as best as one can in the light of the prevailing circumstances. It was clear that the force would function directly under the directions of the Chief of the Army Staff (COAS) and not under the Eastern Army Commander. Nor would it have anything to do with the adjacent Army Corps. This bestowed the greatest freedom of action except for our supply drops and motor transport for which we were dependent on the GOC-in-C Eastern

Command, Lt-General Aurora. So far so good, but when I read the tasks allotted, it shocked me.

SFF was asked to blow up Kaptai Dam and some bridges and communications and in general harass the Pak forces deployed in that area, thus drawing Pak reserves into this area and securing the flank of our assaulting corps. Verbally COAS had said he would be more than satisfied if SFF could achieve these tasks within specified timings. It was obvious that Army Headquarters were not certain about the potential of this force which was much greater than the tasks assigned. Moreover, I was keen that these men achieve something spectacular in their first ever action, to boost up their morale as well as prove to the nation that the money spent on this force in peace time was a worthwhile expenditure.

I met the COAS and protested against this assignment which lacked any worthwhile challenge to inspire my men. He relented somewhat and asked me what were my aspirations.

I said, "Give me the capture of Chittagong Port as my main task. Other tasks like demolition of Kaptai Dam would fall into their proper place as subsidiary tasks. This would give the men a worthwhile challenge and would provide momentum to my operation."

He said, "How would you capture this strongly defended place without Air or Artillery support? You do not even have heavy mortars." I said, "Leave that to us. We shall prove worthy of your trust."

He promised to consider my request later. I felt he wanted to see some proof of our ability in war before assigning such a heavy responsibility to us and I do not blame him. So much adverse propaganda had gone on for years in the Army against the Force that even as fair minded and impartial a Commander as Sam Manekshaw had been affected by it.

Meanwhile I was sent for by the Minister in charge—Mr DP Dhar and I found this a golden opportunity to convince him about our capabilities. I told him that my great desire was to proceed to Dacca by sea after the capture of Chittagong Port, secretly infiltrate 1000 SFF men in Dacca with the help of the Mujeeb Bahini, activate about 2000 Bahini boys already working underground in that city and play havoc with the enemy troops there. This would so undermine the morale of the enemy that he would surrender on the first sight of Indian Army troops in the vicinity. My Mujeeb Bahini leaders were all convinced of the soundness and practicability of this plan to shorten the operations, which we at that time suspected might be prolonged, in order to allow the Pak allies and friends to intervene to save the situation.

I pointed out all this on the map to Mr DP Dhar who promised to press upon the COAS to give me the task of capture of Chittagong initially. I knew that the COAS could be persuaded but not pressurised. And the best persuation would be the proof of our ability. I, therefore, decided to do my utmost to win the spurs, by some spectacular victories right in the beginning.

I had explained the whole plan to my Civilian Chief Mr RN Kao, who had a lot of faith in me. He was, however, sceptical about the results we might ultimately achieve in view of the total lack of Artillery and Air support as well as a lack of understanding that had continued between the Army and the SFF right from the very inception of the concept of SFF. He was not so sure of even the administrative support Army had promised me. I had my own fears on the same grounds but being a born optimist and with faith in God I thought everything would turn out to be alright.

The greatest attributes of Mr Kao was not to interfere in his subordinates' initiatives and to fully support all legitimate action by them. His own intellect, power of quick decision and personal influence in the right quarters was a great asset. His unfailing courtesy and promptness of action left an indelible impression on me and I hoped and prayed that I would not be found wanting in the trust he invariably placed in me.

My biggest tussle was of course with the Air Wing of my organisation who were not prepared to spare even two old helicopters out of their fleet, to be placed under my command for this vital operation. The Director appeared keen to keep them all in the base so that they do not get damaged in war. Men's lives and the success of this operation appeared of secondary importance to this Civilian dignitary than the safety of his helicopters. This is where minds did not meet. My Civilian

Chief ultimately succeeded in getting for me one helicopter with an excellent crew. Imagine a Force of the potential of Special Frontier Force launched into a vital operation with one helicopter where the minimum requirement was six.

Our outstanding successes in spite of these enormous handicaps go to show the spirit which pervaded the Special Frontier Force at this time.

CHAPTER 10

Taming of Tigers

The Special Frontier Force was raised from the inaccessible Northern Hill tribes, soon after the Chinese invasion of India in October 1962. Mr BN Mullick has referred to this force in his book *The Chinese Betrayal—My Years with Nehru*. Essentially these frontier-men were required to help fight the Chinese, if they ever advanced again into Indian territory, by fighting behind their lines as Guerillas.

These men are all physically tough and totally fearless. Believing in rebirth, they treat death as a gateway to a better life in future. This often makes them quite reckless. Their sharp eye and instinctive reaction to danger makes them excellent recruits for Guerilla training. They love modern weapons with great killing power and soon become crack-shots. One thing they detest is to be separated from their weapons. They like to sleep with their light machine-guns and cannot understand handing them over for safe custody into a regular quarter-guard. Some of them may even feel insulted when asked to deposit their weapons in the unit quarter-guard and start suspecting that they are perhaps not trusted by the authoritics. They have enormous lung capacity which, coupled with their extraordinary physical stamina, makes them ideal fighters in high altitudes.

Their totally independent nature with considerable manly pride makes them less amenable to enforced discipline. It was also felt that bringing them under the Army or the Police Act would blunt the very qualities of Independent initiative and decision so vital in a patriotic Guerilla. It was therefore decided to organise this volunteer force as a civilian force working under the administrative control of the Director of Intelligence Bureau—at this time Mr BN Mullick. Their training and deployment in peace and war was to be entrusted to a soldier with an unconventional bent of mind, who could win their confidence and lead them into war if necessary, without the help of a rigid Army code prescribing punishments for various crimes of omission and commission.

The Choice of the Army Headquarters fell on me. I was then commanding an Artillery brigade in a Field Area. I had just come on a well earned leave, when I was summoned to take charge of this unique force. Mr Krishna Menon, the then Defence Minister personally interviewed me in the presence of the Chief of Staff, Lt-General B.M. Kaul, and left me in no doubt about the difficult and hazardous nature of my undertaking. I had always been looking for some such challenge but this was something even beyond my dreams. I was told that disciplining this force, without the help and support of the Army Act would be like the taming of wild tigers and I should be prepared for some injuries in the process.

In retrospect I am happy to say that the fears of the high authorities about the difficulties of disciplining this force were unfounded. It is on record that no force of such diverse origin and composition ever showed better discipline. We had no crime. Everyone was busy training physically and psychologically. There was only one unfortunate case of suicide in the whole force in many years and this was due to the fact that the individual concerned was found unfit to carry out para-jumps in a Medical examination, since he had a malformed ankle and would have broken his legs or spine if allowed to jump. He pleaded before every leader that he should be allowed to jump in spite of his deformity which was not accepted. This highly patriotic, brave and sensitive individual then committed suicide by hanging from a tree.

He left an impression of his feelings on his leaders that even his genuine physical disability would make him look a coward in the eyes of his colleagues since he would not participate in para-jumping—the very first hazard the Force was undertaking. Under such circumstances his life had no meaning.

This was the kind of spirit which the Force had imbibed.

They controlled their love for drinking and gambling at my behest, which removed the major causes of trouble among them. Vigorous dancing and chanting of Buddhist hymns took care of any leisure period they had. The severest punishment was to be paraded before their own communal group, to be chastised, for any unbecoming conduct and the worst threat that a leader could administer to an erring individual was of being produced before myself—the Force Commander, for introspection.

Since the Special Frontier Force were to function in close support of the Indian Army they had to be exercised with the units and formations manning the border, in order to win their confidence. The Army, however, insisted that they be put under their command, trained and disciplined like regular soldiers to be of any use to them. This was not possible and the trouble continued endlessly.

The Army Headquarters ordered an exercise in which they wanted to test the whole force against an Army Brigade in a mountainous terrain. It was obvious that they did not fully appreciate the correct employment of this force. I suggested that about 100 men of SFF would be adequate for the task of tying down the Army Brigade, they did not believe me. Ultimately they were persuaded to agree. The Director of Military Training, a Major General, himself was to direct the exercise and act also as the enemy corps commander. My men trapped him in broad daylight and told their own umpire to record him as having been killed since he was facing their rifles at about five metres. All enemy umpires were full of praise. for their excellent planning and tactics in which they had tied the whole brigade to a most reprehensible defensive posture, destroyed his wireless and line communications, ammunition and supply dumps and forced him to stick to the main highway, inflicting heavy damage whenever he dared patrol away from the road. The Chief umpire showed me his report and congratulated me on the excellent training of my men. But the Army Headquarters tore off this report and sent a hasty letter showing how weak the SFF training was. Simultaneously they charged our exercise enemy, the Army Brigade Commander, for inefficiency in being overwhelmed by such a small force of Guerillas.

It was quite clear that the Army wanted to prove to the Government that SFF must be put under their command to improve their efficiency; the Army Headquarters intimated the Defence Secretary about their assessment of this exercise to ensure that action at political level was initiated.

In some Armies the best technique of denigrating a field commander is to prove him a failure in an exercise which is judged solely by the superior who is bent upon taking revenge against the victim who is so exercised. In this arbitrary game there is no impartial tribunal. Also there is no appeal since the senior is by custom supposed to be the repository of all military wisdom. This was true of our Army also, though I believe things are changing now with more liberal and competent commanders.

My civilian boss Mr B.N. Mullick, one of the most competent civil servants, understood the whole situation very well, after he had the exercise setting and results analysed by some foreign experts. I was terribly depressed to find meanness at such high levels and waited anxiously for an opportunity to prove our worth—preferably in a war. But wars are not of one's own seeking. The next best thing was to run an exercise under the direction of an Army Commander who is not only known for his competence but impartiality. The chance soon presented itself. Lt-General J.S. Dhillon, GOC-in-C Central Command (who was primarily responsible for all the success we had achieved against Pakistan in 1965) was to run an exercise for one of his Divisions where we could fit in our normal role. He was known to be a commander of highest integrity and thoroughness. We participated in this exercise called 'Garuda' and as a result I got the report which helped greatly in restoring our image and acted as a tonic for future effort.

Comments by Lt-General J.S. Dhillon, GOC-in-C:

> The Director of the Exercise reports that the SFF company functioned creditably and achieved the tasks assigned to it and the impact of this force on the enemy was striking in that it seriously handicapped him in his build up.
>
> The military personnel taking part, directing and umpiring in this exercise were greatly impressed by the SFF capabilities. They all feel that the SFF is going to be a great asset in any operations that we undertake.
>
> Everyone knows that you have been the architect of this Force from the time it was conceived. I want to take this opportunity to

> congratulate you on your achievement in organising and training this Force up to such a high standard.

This last para was addressed to me as the Force Commander. Comments by the Director of Exercise 'Garuda':

> This force did very well throughout the exercise. The main reasons for their success are as under:
>
> (a) Their personnel had a thorough knowledge of the ground they were operating on.
>
> (b) They were highly mobile specially at night.
>
> (c) Their raids were carried out with speed and achieved surprise.
>
> (d) Their security was of a high order; when they abandoned a base or a hide out, no traces of their presence there were left behind.
>
> (e) Deceptive measures were adopted extensively by demonstrating at a point other than where they struck.
>
> **Major General**
> *G.O.C. Division*

I thought it would be fruitful to invite Lt-General KP Candeth, PVSM, GOC-in-C Western Command to visit the Force on an exercise and form his own impressions of their ability. General Candeth was an officer with great breadth of vision and candour. I was not so sure about his views on such unconventional forces as the SFF and kept my fingers crossed while he watched an exercise. This is what he had to say:

> ... how impressed I was with all that I saw there. I was particularly struck by the high standard of shooting and physical fitness of the men; their ability to move rapidly over difficult mountainous terrain was an eye opener to me. The maintenance of discipline, when there are no laws and orders and no accepted scale of punishment must be a truly difficult task and I was greatly impressed by the way you and your officers managed to maintain discipline. The cheerfulness of the people is a true indication of the spirit that prevails in the SFF.

Later I had an occasion to invite Lt-General JS Aurora GOC-in-C Eastern Command who was destined to win the historic war of Bangladesh, to visit the Force. He was highly impressed. Writing about the Force he said "I am fully convinced that they are capable of delivering, and will certainly deliver, the goods if and when an opportunity arises. … May I compliment you for all that you have achieved in spite of many difficulties and misunderstandings under which you had to work. I can only say that this could not have been done by a lesser person who lacked your devotion and determination."

This comment was most welcome from a person who knew the genesis of this misunderstanding.

By now the three top Army Commanders appeared convinced of the efficiency of this Force and had expressed confidence in its leadership. The most inspiring message, however, came from General Sam Manekshaw, who visited the Force at my request. He wrote, "It was a wonderful experience and I have seldom felt so elated. Your troops looked to be in excellent heart, extremely fit and with a great deal of motivation. It would be a pleasure for any soldier to get the opportunity of leading such fine men. Without wishing to be patronising, I think a great deal of credit must go to you for having made such a wonderful fighting force out of men from such different areas and surroundings."

The whole atmosphere changed with the arrival of General Manckshaw on the scene. Petty rivalaries between the Army Headquarters and SFF ended at least for the time being. This shrewd Chief was to inspire and drive us into some of the most hazardous operations in our history. We will come to that later.

Para-jump training of these men meant jumping with a parachute from a moving plane accurately into a target area. For men who have not seen a single machine of any kind in their whole life, it is no easy job. I therefore, avoided all sophisticated gadgets for training which our modern Armies use since they frighten a novice. We improvised simple techniques of ground training and waited for the real jumps with fingers crossed. Of all the officers seconded to this volunteer Force from the Army, no one was para-trained or a para-volunteer. Although many officers carried out the ground training for several months with these men, they were all under the impression that they would not have to carry out the real jumps from an aircraft, since they were not para-volunteers and were also of a higher age group for which the Government does not accept the risk and pays no compensation in case of death or injury. I was, therefore, in for a big crisis in my Command.

It is vital for the health of a command structure that the officers must share all hazards with men starting with the training hazards. When I asked for the names of officer volunteers to jump with the men I drew a blank. This was just one day prior to the real jumps. I had always been under the impression that all officers training with the men would lead their men in real jumps. This was a critical situation. Men would never obey the commands of an officer in war if they lose faith in him in peace. It was not that the officers lacked courage. The main reason was that their risk was not covered under Government rules because of their age group and they felt justified in not taking such risks. But for me it was a simple question of either winning the confidence of men or relinquishing command.

This talk of Government not accepting the risks of men above 36 was seriously affecting the men as well. Many of whom were above this age and felt it must indeed be risky to jump after that age, since the Government did not accept the risks. I had only one day left and I could not get Governments decision in one day under any circumstances.

I, therefore, adopted the only course open to me. I addressed all the men the same evening as follows, "Para-jumping is not at all risky. It is one of the pleasantest ways of travelling and closing in on an enemy fresh without any fatigue. It does not need much training and it is safe for all ages. You know I have had no para-training but I shall personally lead every group in jumping from an aircraft unless some other officer volunteers to jump at the head of men after me."

This electrified the whole atmosphere. Every one knew I was more aged than anyone of them. They also knew I had had no training. But when the top commander takes the lead it has a very deep effect.

Now having said all this to the men and enjoyed their shrill war cries, I started thinking of how to carry out the promise I had made to the men. I had only one night to learn the art of jumping and that too from my tea table on the carpet of my drawing room. I requested a junior to teach me the ground role in my drawing room that night and explain the use of cords attached to the parachute. I had seen some of this on the training ground during my visits and always felt sure it was easy. That night everything appeared difficult. Anyway I did a few awkward rolls on my carpet, jumping from my tea table and my instructor took a promise from me that I would never tell anyone I was trained by him. He left me with the words that I should reconsider my decision to jump next day with the men and get regular ground training for a month at least before jumping.

It was not so simple for me. I had to do what I had said if I was to command that Force. I had sent a letter to Mr BN Mullick who was out of his Headquarters, explaining the reason for my decision and requesting for proper compensation to our families in case we died. As an additional precaution I had written a letter to my brother, Dr Gopal Singh MP, later our distinguished ambassador in many countries, to help the family if I died. I jumped as the first man next day and made a perfect landing. Mr BN Mullick on learning of my successful jump sent a message of congratulations to me not only from himself but from Pandit Jawaharlal Nehru, our Prime Minister, as well.

This one jump of mine without training smoothened many of our difficulties with the men as well as the Government. Every one jumped. My driver Havildar Sarup Singh jumped. Cooks jumped. The Quarter-masters jumped. All flaunted their para-badges and walked with pride of men.

Later Mr BN Mullick presented me to the Prime Minister Pandit Jawaharlal Nehru in his Office. I can never forget the kindness with which the PM received me expressing his great desire to jump with me during our next schedule.

We were all proud of working under Mr BN Mullick, this selfless man who matched the talent, the self-sacrifice, sense of patriotism and unparalleled dedication to the work of the Nation, of the leaders of the stature of Jawaharlal Nehru, Sardar Patel and Pandit Pant under whom he served. His incorruptible, austere and tough character, coupled with his towering intellect stood the test of most difficult times and he devised techniques and raised forces which would help defend this country against all odds for a long time to come.

It is most unfortunate that this country soon forgets its geniuses and has no system of properly honouring or utilising the talents of its top experts once they are superannuated and retired.

He has recently died of a heart attack at the age of 78 as a great disciple of Baba Onkarnath. All honour to him. The country has lost a gem of a man.

CHAPTER 11

Launching of 'Operation Eagle'

Movement of Special Frontier Force by air commenced soon after my able Chief of Staff, Colonel Iqbal Singh MC, had sent in his intelligence reports, based on ground reconnaissance and questioning of some Mizo captives detained in Aizawal—the capital of Mizoram. Colonel Iqbal Singh had commanded an infantry brigade in this disturbed area earlier and had done exceedingly well. He had good knowledge of the terrain and the tactics generally employed by Mizo rebels. I had a lot of faith in this Officers' competence and assessment. The only reason he had not picked up the rank of a Brigadier was that he was too outspoken and honest. There was a clash of personalities between him and his next senior and naturally being junior he lost. I was fortunate in having such a dependable officer as my Chief of Staff.

Movement by Air was followed by movement in motor transport along the Road Silchar-Aizawal-Lungleh. Unfortunately the bridges across *Chongs* on the road between Lungleh and Demagiri, the border post selected by me for my Headquarters, and main base were broken. All equipment and stores had, therefore, to be carried by men. Many stores and main wireless station were left behind at Lungleh in the hope of being moved to Demagiri when the bridges got repaired.

The movement to and fro between Demagiri and Lungleh continued day and night and created an impression of a big force being assembled to assault Chittagong from the East.

Demagiri is located along a ridge called Sirte-Tlang about 2000 feet high, running North-South, parallel to the Bangladesh border. I selected three other posts along this ridge, viz., Marpara, to the North and Bornapansuri, Jarulchari to the South of Demagiri where I wanted to concentrate SFF columns for their assaults within Bangladesh.

Stores and supplies were dropped by air on these posts as well as further South over a long period, creating the illusion of a big force being concentrated. This illusion was further strengthened by constant movement of men and material between Demagiri and other posts North and South. My own daylight reconnaissances in a Major General's uniform by paddle boats in River Karnaphuli, in full view of hundreds of Mizos, going to meet the civil officials in Demagiri town and stationing of the only one helicopter we had at Demagiri helipad confirmed the illusion, that about one Division was already concentrated at Demagiri. One Bengali Member of National Assembly, MNA, who was to accompany us told several people that he had himself counted 8000 troops at Demagiri alone, where we never had more than 400 men.

Rangamati town was the first big objective but it needed a fleet of boats to open the only artery of communication, i.e., River Karnaphuli. This river criss-crossed across three hill ranges up to this town, all of which were manned by tough Pathans and wily Mizos and supported by all the local Chakma tribesmen. The town of Barkal almost halfway to Rangamati had particularly strong defences sited on dominating heights with well dug in bunkers. The area *Barkal-Subalong* was vital for the enemy.

The enemy was naturally sensitive to any thrust along this line. We soon found that Barkal got reinforced and considerable reinforcements moved up North on the ridges both sides of the river.

We started collecting river boats but found only small ones capable of taking no more than four to six men. Mostly they were two-men fishing boats.

Tactics

It was clear from the beginning that the enemy defensive positions, sited and stocked to delay our advance, were not going to be evacuated by lightly armed Guerillas. They would need powerful commando assaults supported by heavy mortars or Artillery and Air. Surprise, the best weapon of Guerillas, would pay handsome dividends but in this situation surprise could only be effected by unexpected mobility and that depends upon the availability of a helicopter fleet. I only had one helicopter for casualty clearance. Our mobility was, therefore, severely restricted.

I decided upon a mixture of Commando-cum-Guerilla tactics and planned to use two columns at a time, one of which would act as the Anvil and the second as a Hammer. The less mobile Anvil force was to follow in general the course of the River Karnaphuli and the most mobile Hammer force would strike and crush the enemy outposts on to the Anvil at Barkal. Subalong and finally Rangamati after which a fresh strategy would be adopted depending upon the situation then prevailing. This was termed by me the Anvil-Hammer tactics. Anvil was called the Sucking Anvil since I wanted extensive Guerilla ambushes around this position, sucking in and destroying any parties moving in or out of it. This was carefully explained to all field commanders. Unfortunately some of them were newly posted from the Army and could not comprehend the intricacies of Guerilla warfare. They however, did their best and learnt by some costly mistakes.

The first requirement in this case was to cross River Karnaphuli, form a large enough bridgehead across the river, within Bangladesh territory from where to launch the assaulting Commandos. An opposed river crossing right in the beginning of an attack is extremely dangerous and avoided by all soldiers but we had no alternative. The river had to be crossed and the opposite side was reported to be manned by the enemy.

There were certain inevitable delays in the preparation of the assault Force moving across several miles of thick forest. To save time I decided to give the task of forming a bridgehead across the river to my Force Headquarters who had only one company available for this assault at Demagiri. We used 19 local boats made available to us on payment by the collector at Demagiri. Fortunately, the enemy post on the opposite bank of the river had just been withdrawn by the enemy quite unknown to us and the crossing was silent and unopposed. The troops fanned out and made room for assaulting companies to assemble and organise.

Although I accompanied the assault group, I decided to give a free hand to the company commander, who carried out this difficult operation of capturing a bridgehead very well. Morale rose high.

Freshly caught fish was fried and served for breakfast along with mugs full of hot tea. I gave out the orders to all commanders from Bangladesh territory and every one was excited about the prospects of a Force being launched in its first ever action in war. Commanders briefed their own commands and with a swift movement every one walked off to his designated task. The launching and the orders session appeared perfect and with high hopes I rowed back to my Headquarters to have a peaceful lunch in my bunk.

I then flew in my helicopter to the Headquarters of the South Column, gave orders for assault and flew further South to evacuate Lt-Colonel N Whig who had broken his knee by slipping during a night movement and was in agony. I had very high hopes in this gallant officer, whom I had personally picked up for some of the toughest tasks in the Force. He had completed reconnaissance giving excellent assessments but destiny did not permit him to participate and win a decoration which I was certain he would win. The officer had to be evacuated to a base hospital in India.

CHAPTER 12

Forging the Anvil

This should not be taken in the literal military sense of a powerfully manned defensive position, to which the enemy forces are guided and crushed by a sledge hammer. The Anvil of our creation was simply to develop an idea in the enemy mind, of our major assault and effort being concentrated, onto the focal point of the enemy line of communication, to which he was naturally sensitive. This was *Barkal-Subalong* area controlling the defiles along *River Karnaphuli.* SFF assaults mounted in the close vicinity of this sensitive area were bound to draw his reserves into this area from his main base *Rangamati* which was our first objective. Simultaneously our Northern columns were to strike with speed. Pushing some retreating enemy Northern outposts onto this position and annihilating others which decided to oppose us. Our Guerilla Force was neither equipped nor trained to take on major defensive positions of the enemy. We had infiltrated our armed cadres to join hands with the freedom fighters within the enemy's important defensive bases of *Rangamati* and *Chittagong.* They were to synchronise their attacks with our striking columns causing fear and despondency in enemy mind of being under attack from within and without. Thus encouraging him to run away and save his life or get killed.

Large number of Guerillas were to keep this critical area constantly under fire, lay ambushes, annihilate enemy patrols, cut off their communication and supplies from within causing complete chaos. The enemy defendants were bound to ask for reinforcements from Rangamati and Chittagong. This is what we wanted.

The Central Column under Major Surat Singh VSM which was assigned this task was split into two sub-columns, which advanced towards Barkal in a pincer move. The sub-columns were commanded successively by Major Surat Singh, Major SR Bhatia, Major BS Thapa and Major SDS Sanial. They were to clear the enemy outposts at Dhanubak, Dighalchari and Baraital and then move South towards

Barkal. Local boats arranged by Major HC Sharma were pushed along the river to be available to this column for moving South along the river or crossing it to wipe out the posts on Barkal Pahar. The NCO incharge of this flotilla went fearlessly at top speed past his rendezvous and right opposite an enemy position at night where he was challenged, and shot at, though seriously wounded he managed to reverse all boats and speeded them towards the rendezvous where the boats reached safely. This gallant NCO collapsed after completing his task and fell into the river. His dead body was discovered in a creek a few days later and cremated with great honour.

This Force made a ferocious attack at Dhanubak, Dighalchari and Baraital capturing these posts and killing all who dared oppose them. They also captured LMGs, rifles and some grenades. Now they came under very heavy fire first from the opposite side of the river and then from close quarters. A senior gallant leader who was standing boldly guiding his men got shot in the stomach. The casualty of this brave leader and the unexpected volume of mortar and machine-gun fire, completely unnerved the inexperienced officers and men, who were equipped with light weapons. The Army Officer incharge started seeking my permission to withdraw from the recently occupied posts and to burn the cypher documents in a typical military style. He was new and had not imbibed the basic principles of Guerilla warfare. As a Guerilla you never hold ground nor take up defensive position. You can clear it by annihilating the enemy or dominate it by fire. But you are never static. You should be highly mobile. You withdraw when the situation so demands and there is no shame in it. Only a stupid fool stays put to get killed.

But the worst that happened here was that the Officers carried out a hasty unplanned withdrawal, demoralising the rank and file, who had suffered only seven casualties all of whom were evacuated, and the medical officer Major Romesh Chandra was sent to treat the casualties as far forward as possible. Unfortunately this wounded leader died. He was cremated with appropriate honours at Demagiri, the Force Headquarters. Other casualties soon recovered in our hospital.

When I had returned to Demagiri from the enemy side of the river where I had given out the orders. I was sure all ranks were in fine trim. But this was their first action. Most officers were newly posted to the force and did not know the men. Mentally they were still rigidly following the normal tactics of war taught to a soldier. Guerilla warfare was something quite new and not an easily understood concept when applied in this sem-military fashion of tackling enemy strongholds with light weapons. I had my doubts and was keeping my fingers crossed when I got the news first of their outstanding action at Dighalchari and then their forced withdrawal back to the point of start.

With a small escort I recrossed the river in a small boat and was shocked to see the whole sub-column back in the area of the bridgehead from where they had started. I was furious and upbraided the young officers and leaders for their cowardly conduct in the face of a demoralised enemy. I talked to the officers, leaders and men separately and sent them back with a better idea of their own potential in Guerilla tactics. They realised their mistakes and promised never to repeat them again. They told me later that this pep talk in the battlefield did them a world of good. This to my mind was the most crucial moment of our role in this war. Any mishandling of the situation here could have downgraded our potential to a mere nuisance value which the authorities expected from us. I had formed a completely different impression of our capabilities and was not prepared to accept this degradation. I knew my officers and the leaders of this Force were imbued with the same spirit. These very men under command of the very same leaders later worked miracles. But this was a moment of great anguish and disappointment for me. Success in this test brought me personally great elation. This group got well established along the eastern ridge and so threatened enemy troops on the western bank that they shrieked for help and told their higher headquarters that thousands of troops were facing them. This was highly exaggerated assessment by them. I used to hear their (Pakistani) wailing after getting tuned to their frequencies. The replies from the headquarters exhorted them to stand up as Mujahids (defending religion) and assuring them that reinforcements were on their way. Some of these reinforcements never reached since they were attacked and drowned en route.

The other column was sent in an encircling move to trap all enemy around Barkal, under the command of Lt-Colonel B.K. Narayan, an officer with good deal of courage and imagination. He was to wipe out the enemy posts at Nirak Para and Jailan Para and then move towards the Hill 1183 south of Barkal. This column fought very bravely and cleared the enemy posts but then unfortunately got ensconced in a nearby locality, surrounded on all sides by nullahs which gave false sense of security where I suppose they wanted to make a base for further adventure.

The enemy soon discovered their predeliction and started harassing and laying booby traps around them. Despite my urgent messages they were not making a move in the direction of their objective south of Barkal, which would have relieved pressure on the centre column and forced the enemy to withdraw from Barkal. By now the enemy position at point 1183, south of Barkal was reinforced and further strengthened. I was able to extricate Lt-Colonel Narayan from this trap by landing my helicopter in the middle of his position, in spite of his protests that the place was under fire and the landing highly risky.

It was at this stage that our Air Force accepted my request and rocketed this enemy strong point. The rocket attack was watched by me and Lt-Colonel AS Assar at close quarters. It was deadly accurate. I sent congratulations to these excellent airmen and asked Lt-Colonel Assar to clear and enter Barkal. Lt-Colonel Assar, still uncertain of enemy designs, was amazed to see Barkal civilians coming in their decorated boats to pick him up ceremoniously from the opposite bank. The enemy had cleared Barkal leaving behind some arms and ammunition which we duly captured. The capture of Barkal was a great morale booster for all of us.

Our Air Battleship

Knowing that this was perhaps the only chance when the Air Force would provide us some support, I ordered that our one and only ME 4 Helicopter should be made into a 'Battleship of the Air' with some of its rear and front parts removed and with a light machine-gun mounted in the rear behind sand bags. I was more than satisfied when our contraption was ready for use. We could fire weapons, throw grenades or roll barrels filled with petrol which would start uncontrollable fires in the right places. My 'Battleship of the Air' was hated by the enemy who fired everything he had on it, including mortar bombs. In fact every time I travelled in it, which was almost daily. I would hear the bullets hitting its bottom as well as the rotor blades on the top, causing vibrations, which got drowned in the din of this infernal machine and it would continue on its journey totally unharmed and unconcerned. At the end of the war this helicopter had become a good museum piece. Our civilian Air Chief almost fainted on seeing its condition and made a historic pronouncement, "My God! what callous waste of a good plane."

CHAPTER 13

Securing of Barkal-Subalong Base

Immediately after the rocket strike on enemy bunker holding us up, we attacked to clear the features dominating *Barkal-Subalong* defile through which River Karnaphuli flowed. Men were in high spirits and soon cleared the area. While Lt-Colonel Assar was making a victorious entry into Barkal town mounted in a highly decorated boat, produced by the local reception committee; Lt-Colonel Narayan was assembling his local boat Armada to take Subalong by surprise. Subalong was a tough proposition, being, flanked by a well-defended high feature.

I sent my congratulations to Lt-Colonel Assar by wireless. We were now holding the key to the capture of *Rangamati*, the main *Mizo* cantonment, where Mr Laldenga, their leader, lived with his family, provided we could clear *Subalong* first.

At this stage we received this wireless message from Field Marshal Manekshaw:

> For Gen UBAN from SAM MANEKSHAW. I am very happy with your progress and results achieved. Well-done and keep it up. Convey my appreciation and best wishes all ranks. Best of Luck.

This was most heartening. The Field Marshal was himself following with deep interest every move we made. I know his computer like brain would miss no detail anywhere; and while not interfering in day-to-day functioning would make the best use of each one of his commanders.

Mr R.N. Kao kept the Prime Minister informed about the progress of my Force. Because of its peculiar nature every one appeared to be interested in this Force. No one expected much from this ill equipped small body of men. Our exploits, therefore, made larger than life impact. Mr Kao sent me the following message:

> Congratulations on good progress made. Wish you all success. Am keeping my superior informed.

Lt-Colonel K.B. Joshi, a recently arrived Gurkha officer, was pressing hard in the Central area and at dawn found himself facing heavily dug and fortified Bunker's pouring out tremendous volume of fire. We could not afford to attack prepared positions in daylight, but despite my instructions to the contrary, this gallant officer charged the position in the regular Army style and got two of his men wounded. He was ordered to break contact and move from another direction. He soon captured a major enemy post of Rangi Para along with three supporting positions. I conveyed my congratulations to him and as a special expression of my appreciation for this brave action, I visited him presonally, carrying with me the special brand of tobacco he always smoked in his pipe. Nothing could have pleased him more.

Reconnaissance showed that before we could clear Subalong, it was absolutely vital to attack and clear Khagrachari, a base which supported Barkal and Subalong being equidistant from both. This target consisted of ten enemy positions with a rivulet swollen like a lake on one side and high hills on the other. The positions were all along a row facing the hillside, from which they expected enemy attack. Some of these positions supported each other and were well sighted.

This was to prove one of our costliest ventures. I immediately set about raising a new column for this task by withdrawing companies from the columns which were resting after action. 43 Coy known for its courage and resolution was added to the 15 and 16 Coys. Leader Chhawan, a great dare devil, was appointed the column leader along with the Company Commander S.K. Suri, another brave officer. I gave a pep talk to officers and men and was certain of success.

Just at this crucial moment when all preparations had been made for our attack, I received a message to reach Delhi immediately for some operational consultations with my civilian superior. First I thought of sending in a representation to get myself excused from this vexatious journey but knowing my boss, I was sure he would not send for me unless the matter was really important.

On arrival in Delhi I found that some of my Guerilla coys, which should have been dispatched to me in Bangladesh had actually been sent elsewhere on routine duties, which even the territorial Army could perform. I was livid and went straight to Mr Kao's house. On enquiring I found that this was done by Army Headquarters and the highest authorities had agreed to this move. He further suggested that since men had reached their destination, many hundreds of miles away, getting them back at that stage was out of question. I was not prepared to accept this and suggested that I meet the Army Chief to get this decision reversed. He said, he had no objection but had no hopes of getting these men back in a short time.

Anyway I met the Chief and as anticipated he saw a lot of weight in my argument and promised immediate orders for their return. This is one quality in Field Marshal Manekshaw which sets him apart as a Field Commander. If, he is convinced you are right, he would not mind rescinding his own orders. I came back quite happy.

During this meeting General Manekshaw congratulated me profusely and named me "My Commander in Chief of the East". Both the Vice Chief and the Deputy Chief of Army Staff hugged me while congratulating me on my exploits.

The Army Chief promised to extend the scope of my operational instructions by making the capture of Chittagong Port and Town as my responsibility. He also suggested that I should shift from the Eastern half of Chittagong Hill Tracts to the Western half, for ease of administration, since I would thus be close to the Corps Headquarters. Knowing the inflexible minds and the petty jealousies which might erupt by my proximity to that headquarter I wanted to avoid that as one would avoid plague. I firmly declined this offer. He gave his charming smile and said, "You Rogue!".

He knew I would not bite that bait. The catastrophe had been averted and I felt really relieved and happy.

This exhilaration was short lived. I learnt from a wireless message—by my Chief of Staff, that the *Thunder Bolt* had been launched successfully resulting in twenty-one deaths on our side. 'Thunder Bolt' was the code name for our Assault on Khagrachari which I had planned with such great care. They could have waited for a couple of days when I would have returned from Delhi and carried it out under my personal supervision. It may not have made much difference to the number of casualties because it was a tough target. But, at least I would have had the satisfaction of checking every detail myself. Mr Kao being a man of conscience, was highly apologetic for having pulled me out of my operational area at a critical moment.

The leaders were too restive and could not wait. They even forgot the basic precaution of attacking either at dusk or dawn. They attacked when the sun was up and all enemy posts well alerted. My men were getting over-confident, so were their leaders. Chhawan himself narrated the attack with his mischievous smile as if it was a big picnic party. They attacked all positions simultaneously in broad daylight, with light machineguns blazing in their hands, after the hand-grenades thrown by them had shaken the enemy. Their blood curdling war cries and long daggers dangling by their sides, unnerved the enemy, some of whom jumped into the lake waters to avoid cold steel. None was left alive except three Pathans who hid themselves in the bushes and exposed themselves after two days fasting. They were promptly sent back to the nearest Army unit, since we entertained no prisoners, for lack of facilities. Twenty-one brave men paid the price for this outstanding victory. Their courage and supreme sacrifice inspired my men to acts of greater daring later and their names will remain enshrined in the pages of history for ever.

I learnt at Delhi how the Pakistanis had attacked all our Airfields in the West and the damages caused in Amritsar. Delhi was having its alerts regularly.

My wife was alone at home and spent all her time praying. Praying for my safety. Praying for our sons safety. My son Major Gurdeep Singh Uban was fighting near Ferozepur as an Artillery Officer. I was told he was doing exceedingly well. None of us knew what was happening to the others. My daughter Harsharan was serving as a Medical Officer in a military hospital along with her husband Squadron Leader K.K. Mishra, a specialist in Surgery. Later, my younger son Jagdip Singh Uban also joined the Air Force. It would be clear that my whole family was serving the Nation and was totally committed. It should not be difficult to understand a soldier's love for peace.

Although my wife was happy to see me back safe in Delhi she knew I was going back to the worst operational area in a couple of days with a heavier assignment. Her anxieties grew with every passing minute and I could be of no help. In any case I was busy meeting the Army Command, the civilian secretariat and the Minister in charge—Mr D.P. Dhar.

Mr D.P. Dhar who had been made Minister in charge of the Bangladesh operation was a very dynamic personality. He exuded charm and was on extremely familiar terms with our Chief, General Manekshaw. He was constantly meeting the Chief, Lt-General Aurora, Mr Kao, the Bangladesh Provisional Government, youth leaders of Bangladesh, and hundreds of others connected with this operation.

Very fond of his whisky, he was horrified to find that I did not drink. He appeared more shocked later when he invited me for lunch to his house at 13 Safdarjang Road, New Delhi, and my boss told him that I was a vegetarian. He could not understand a soldier who was a vegetarian and a teetotaller.

After my first interview I could assess that Mr Dhar was a determined man who relentlessly pursued his objectives. He was known to be a communist who had completely won the confidence of the Prime Minister, Mrs Indira Gandhi. He was also largely held instrumental in consummating the long-term IndoSoviet treaty of friendship which had paid the country so well during the Bangladesh War in neutralising the threat of American Seventh Fleet in the Bay of Bengal. This was a period of his ascendence when he could do no wrong. For my present task his patronage was very important.

During this meeting in the Minister's house I spent about one hour with him on my Operational Map and told him my entire plan of capturing Chittagong and thence proceeding by sea secretly to enter Dacca, where about two thousand Mujeeb Bahini boys were already awaiting our arrival. We could then with the help of these patriots create such chaotic conditions that their Army formations in and around Dacca would be forced to surrender to the first Indian Army troops appearing on the scene. In fact, my hope was to accept surrender before the arrival of the Indian Army units. This part had been rehearsed with the Mujeeb Bahini boys and Sheikh Faza-l-ul-Haq Moni was confident, because of his extensive local knowledge and control of his cadres within Dacca, that we would succeed outstandingly and create history. Both of us were chronic optimists and here our optimism was based on some highly favourable circumstances.

The Minister listened to me with rapt attention and said, "You think you could accomplish this?" When I said, "Yes", he said he would speak to General Manekshaw and help me get these tasks allotted to me if I continued to show sufficient progress, or if and when the Indian Army ran into unforeseen difficulties.

I was more than satisfied with assurance but was not so sure of the reaction of the Army Chief about my plans for Dacca. I had not mentioned this to him and was going to do so only on capture of Chittagong when he would be in a proper frame of mind. He had already promised my first ambition—the capture of Chittagong. I could keep my fingers crossed and hope for the best.

On my way back from Delhi by air I met Group Captain Latte and Squadron Leader Verma of the Indian Air Force at Kumbhigram and explained to them the targets, I wanted *Rangamati* and *Kaptai* rocketed, besides the heights near *Barkal*. They were highly enthusiastic and helpful. They said they could rocket and strafe all the targets on the dates I wanted with four *Hunter* aircrafts. They said they had no other engagement on those dates. I was very happy.

On reaching my Headquarters I phoned Lt-General Sagat Singh, the Corps Commander, whose corps flank I was protecting. He said he would await my formal written request and gave no hopes of meeting my demand in spite of the fact that the Air Force Tactical Headquarters had assured me they were free on those dates. Ultimately no air support came. General Manekshaw's exhortions also had no effect. Our insignificant Force appeared to have acquired the status of a comparable Force. Competing in speed of advance with neighbouring IV Army Corps of three divisions, comprising about 60,000 men, with considerable armour and heavy guns. Since this corps controlled all air strikes, they denied them to us so that we are delayed and they reach *Chittagong* earlier to receive its surrender. Pettiness of mind is not infrequent even in the life and death struggle of a Nation.

Serious attempts were also being made to put Mujeeb Bahini and at this time even the Special Frontier Force under Lt-General Sarkar, a nominee of Mr D.P. Dhar ostensibly to coordinate all Mukti Bahini and Guerilla effort under the Eastern Command, but in actual fact to remove the thorn of an independent command which was doing exceedingly well in comparison with flanking formations.

I signalled my refusal to work under the rigid codes of Army Command to Mr Kao. Knowing that neither the SFF nor Mujeeb Bahini would be prepared to serve under any other military commander, this petty intrigue was scotched by my superior and he assured me of an independent role.

The Indian Army was now pressing hard and every commander was keen to reach Dacca first. The IV Army Corps which was fighting on our flank had the best chances, being nearest to Dacca and having considerable air support.

The Special Frontier Force had established itself in the heart of Chittagong Hill Tracts. The north column was sending consistent good news of its progress. I decided to despatch about 200 Mujeeb Bahini boys to the South to threaten *Kaptai* before attacking *Rangamati.* Sheikh Fazal-ul-Haq Moni, the nephew of Sheikh Mujeeb, had arrived to accompany me to Chittagong and Dacca in accordance with the plan I had formulated and rehearsed with his boys who had already reached Dacca.

India had recognised Bangladesh Government soon after the blatant declaration of war by Pakistan. We celebrated the new status of Bangladesh as a sovereign republic. Mr Moni and some others made feeling references to the role India was paying in their liberation and after my speech the Bengali young men sang and danced.

Next morning the Mujeeb Bahini boys left for their assigned tasks. They were very young and inexperienced and I was apprehensive about their fate. I was horrified to learn later that in order to hide their identity some even dropped their weapons in the river when challenged while crossing in small boats—they, however, retrieved their honour by later challenging the fleeing Mizos across the same river and recovering some weapons from them.

I flew by helicopter to Lungleh to meet the wounded men of SFF in the Advance Military Hospital. In spite of their condition they were full of cheer and lay quiet like wounded tigers. No moaning, no complaints, but a gleam of smile on their faces and all keen to go back to their self-imposed task of showing the enemy their mettle by coming to grips with him.

Soon after I received a wireless message from Colonel Narayan that his attack launched along River Karnaphuli in rickety boats had surprised the enemy and he had captured *Subalong*. I sent my congratulation and 'Well done' to him. With the capture of *Subalong* we had sealed the withdrawal of enemy posts located along the *Kasalong Khal*, their main route of communication to *Rangamati*. The *Anvil* of *Barkal-Subalong* in our hands was now ready to receive the fugitives who survived the *Hammer* column pushing them Southwards along the same route. Trap had been sprung and there was no hope for the enemy to escape.

General Manekshaw sent us another signal of congratulation:

> GEN UBAN from COAS
> Well done and keep up good work
> Expecting big things from you.

We now received some 81-mm mortars, recoilless (RCL) guns and some BMGs without amnunition. Mortar ammunition for our mortars was not available in any ammunition depot. Only a few rounds which would not last a rapid fire for a couple of hours was all that could be scrounged from various sources, all of whom expressed helplessness. Every round was, therefore, precious and was fired for guaranteed effect. RCL guns came in handy against enemy boats and vehicles. BMGs were used mostly for surprise effect.

We also received Motor Board Engines at long last, though all of them proved unserviceable. In any case they would have made a lot of noise and we were entirely dependent upon surprise. Paddle boats of the local variety were the only ones we could use but they had mostly been commandeered by the enemy and we were left with only our own ingenious improvisations.

All available heavier weapons were frequently switched around mostly by the one helicopter to assist companies that were needing them most. The commanders deprived of these naturally groused but I had little time for this. In fact I ordered that my helicopter would lift rations to, and evacuate casualties from, the column which was making fast progress. The slow and static columns would have to wait for their turn even if it meant great hardship for them. The *Centre* column on one occasion missed its ration supply for three days and were forced to live on freshly caught fish which was very meagre, since they did not know the technique of catching fish and had no appropriate implements. Knowing that the only chance of getting replenished was to attack the enemy successfully and capture his rations or in any case lay claims to priority treatment because of success in operations, they attacked two enemy positions one after another on a half empty stomach and succeeded. I rushed myself with a helicopter full of supplies and joined them in their first hot meal after several days.

Ration supply, all of which had to be first dropped at selected points by our own Air Force (a considerable part of these supplies could never he retrieved since it got dropped in the middle of a river or a deep ravine), was then lifted on manpack basis as well as by the one helicopter for fast advancing columns. This along with ammunition supply was a major administrative problem and kept my staff on tenter-hooks most of the time.

To this would be added some avoidable problems by the parent organisations in Delhi. Once a signal officer who was a known bad hat was posted to the Special Frontier Force (SFF) to fill a vacancy. Everyone knows, my Chief Signal Officer, Major Dutta (an extremely efficient and balanced signals officer), told me, that this Officer would only make a nuisance of himself wherever he went, yet he was sent to us in the thick of the battle and true to style he refused to obey his superiors. We had no time for Court Martial. We sent him back posthaste but it wasted a lot of our valuable time.

General Manekshaw had promised me Air support during my recent visit to Delhi and had asked the Director of Military Operations, General Gill, an excellent soldier, to work out the details but nothing came of it. The Command and Corps Headquarters claimed every single air strike for their own use and gave us only pin-pricks. We reconciled ourselves to this situation and relied even more on our own ingenuity and courage.

CHAPTER 14

The Hammer Strikes: Exploits of North Column

While the centre column was busy consolidating its position in *Barkal-Subalong* area, thus forming the *Anvil*, the North column under Colonel PC Purkyastha was concentrating along Mizoram border at *Marpara*. This column had the most difficult task of destroying all the enemy posts along *Kasalong Khal*, a rivulet joining River Karnaphuli at *Subalong* which was swollen to a formidable stretch of water. There were enemy posts consisting of Mizos strengthened by Pathans and Baluchis who held this whole territory under ransom. Colonel Purkyastha was a tall, well built and daring officer who ably assisted by Major RK Malhotra and Major GS Man as subcolumn commanders carried out this assignment outstandingly. Leader *Rathu* was a tower of strength to him in this adventure.

The enemy once surprised by sudden and ferocious attacks was kept constantly on the run. Posts of *Mahmuam Rului, Masalang, Ganga Ram Rh, Tintillia* and *Mershiya* fell quickly in succession. The two sub-columns joined up at *Dussuri-Khal* junction and proceeded via *Mahiliya* to *Myanimukh-Khal* junction.

Passage to Myanimukh was through a vast stretch of water. Colonel Purkyastha, who had been advancing on top speed, wanted some rest for his men at this stage but I promised him rest and reorganisation only on capture of *Myanimukh*. In actual fact he could not rest even if I were to allow it since his coy at Mershiya was counter-attacked and had suffered some casualties by enemy 81 mm mortars. The enemy was severely mauled. They left 6 Pathan and 4 Mizo dead bodies and carried four jeep-loads of casualties.

I was keen to remove our own 10 wounded men in a helicopter. It was arranged that one helicopter would be sent to them at a fixed time, which would be guided to their site by a smoke signal, to be set up by the SFF boys. I thought of accompanying the pilot, Flight Lieutenant *Parves Jamasji* on his first flight into the enemy territory when the battle was going on. My presence amongst men who were fighting so valiantly would, I thought, be a great morale booster and the quick evacuation of casualties by helicopter would be highly appreciated by everyone.

Colonel Iqbal, my chief of staff, tried to disuade me from this hazardous venture. As he put it, "A helicopter in war is like a sitting duck for enemy fighters. Our helicopter is old in service and the engine itself may conk out in enemy territory which would make matters worse."

He actually offered to go himself if I thought it necessary for a senior officer to accompany the first sortie within enemy territory.

The seniormost SFF leader JK came running from his bunker when he heard that I was going into the battle zone to retrieve our casualties in a helicopter. He remonstrated with me about the wisdom of my decision although he agreed it would boost up the morale of men endlessly. But he asked, "What will happen to the whole operation if you get shot down along with your helicopter?"

I was getting tired of sitting in my Headquarters bunker and needed some fresh air and this was the best opportunity. I also badly wanted to reconnoitre the area of further advance by Colonel Purkyastha, which was a veritable nightmare. Moreover I wanted to discuss the future operational plan with the Column Commander, which is best done from a vantage point on the affected ground.

Anyway I got into the helicopter to the delight of Flight Lieutenant Parves Jamasji and he started the machine. We followed the course of the hill range within our own territory as long as we could, since we intended shortening the period of our stay in enemy territory to the minimum. When Jamasji reached the point of departure for the enemy territory on his map, he just said, "Sir, we have now entered the enemy territory". My heart started beating faster as I scanned the earth below for the smoke signal which was to guide us on to the rendezvous with our own men. This happened to be the morning meal time and one could see many columns of smoke willowing up in the distance. We did not know which one belonged to us. We had made a bloomer in selecting smoke as our signal at meal time. We did not know there was habitation in our target area. Nothing could be done now.

Just then Jamasji said, "Sir, I can hear the enemy fighter pilots who say they have spotted our helicopter." I said, "Do not worry. Go straight for the smoke in that area (pointing my stick towards a smoke column in the nearest copse of trees)."

As we reached the smoke that I had indicated, I saw some of our men running towards a hut and coming lower we recognised their dress and tried to land on a circular patch of land surrounded on all sides except one with water. Jamasji touched the machine down and kept the engine running. We dismounted and made for the trees some distance away to avoid any fighter or mortar fire.

Colonel Purkyastha was waiting for me there along with his other Group Oficers. The Leader had brought one ripe pineapple for me to eat. I felt tempted since this was the first fresh fruit I had seen in weeks but I thought of taking it to my Headquarters Mess so that my staff officers could also share this delicacy with me.

While the wounded were getting loaded in the helicopter I discussed future plans with Colonel Purkyastha over a hot cup of tea which they had brewed quickly in my honour. The wounded had to be brought from a distant hut and it took quite a bit of time. Jamasji was fuming because of this delay and his fear of the enemy fighters of which I was no less conscious.

The helicopter soon got ready to move and I left the officers and men of North column in excellent spirit. Now they knew that we could evacuate casualties as well as replenish their ammunition with a helicopter in no time. This visit was a great morale booster for everyone including myself. Officers and men in my own Headquarters looked at me with greater reverence from that day onwards. We soon returned to our Headquarters after dropping our wounded at our Forward Hospital at *Lungleh*.

I cannot fathom the reason why the enemy fighters after spotting my helicopter did not attack it. It was one of the many miracles we experienced in this war.

The Field Marshal Honours Us

Pleased with our daily successes in relentless persuit of the enemy, Field Marshal Manekshaw sent a new 'instruction' to me setting the capture of *Chittagong Port* and Town as our objective. There was great rejoicing in my Headquarters on this new honour. The Army Chief had recognised our worth after thoroughly testing our mettle. It was a most unusual recognition, to ask a force trained only in Guerilla warfare and capable of fielding no more than 800 lightly armed men into the battle field at any one time, to destroy the defences of approximately 3000 Mizos trained by the Chinese, deployed in depth for the protection of Rangamati and Chittagong and then chase the Pakistan Army Brigade group from their vital ground of *Chittagong* and capture it.

That day we asked Flight Lieutenant *Jamasji* to cut the pineapple I had brought from the battlefield and after eating the first piece himself to distribute the remainder to other officers in the Mess. I wanted to highlight the brave act of Jamasji in helping evacuate casualties by helicopter and to inspire officers to carry out some of the most hazardous tasks that awaited them. I had nothing better than a pineapple to do it with. The same day I sent recommendation for the immediate award of Vir Chakra to this courageous officer and the Army Chief confirmed the award by an immediate signal—an excellent Army Procedure which puts new life into a Force.

The ceremonies over, I started thinking of occupying *Rangamati*, the most important communication centre, north of *Chittagong* which was the key to the capture of *Chittagong* as well as the famous *Kaptai Dam*.

As luck would have it just at this time all those three important objectives of Rangamati, Kaptai and Chittagong were removed from the responsibility of the Indian Air Force. *Chittagong* being an important objective for the Navy, was immediately dominated by the Indian Naval Air Wing, which posed serious problems of coordination with my commandos, on their way to capture this port. But *Rangamati* and *Kaptai* were outside the range of Naval Aircraft at that time. I therefore requested that our Air Strike Force at Kumbhigram be ordered to take on these targets to smoothen our advance.

Many of my signals were just filed. Every one said. "He can do without air support which we urgently need in and around *Dacca*". So the expected happened. Although the Army Chief arranged with the Navy to give me air support it failed to materialise.

At this time our second helicopter also started functioning. The enemy from *Subalong* had withdrawn to *Rangamati* but many posts along *Kasalong Khal* still held out. I felt that rushing some men close to *Rangamati* to its north-west by helicopter would encircle the town and along with the Mujeeb Bahini boys already infiltrated, could scare the enemy to leave for *Chittagong*. Time was running out. On the same day, therefore, I sent two helicopter-loads of men in the forests northwest of *Rangamati*. They were fired at with mortars but no one was hurt and the helicopter carried back some pieces of bomb metal which had penetrated its not so thick skin. My Guerillas dispersed according to a well-rehearsed plan and were now surrounding Rangamati, where a few of our Mujeeb Bahini boys had already infiltrated.

Perfidy of the Corps Headquarters

Just at this stage when we stood poised to take Rangamati came a signal from the Corps Headquarters that we need not capture Rangamati which was going to be done by Mukti Bahini Command (working under this Corps). I was told that the Provisional Government wanted Mukti Bahini to capture this important town, ostensibly for some political reasons. I knew there was no one from Mukti Bahini Force in that area and they wanted to cash in on our efforts. I therefore signalled back to say, "SFF men are surrounding the area and have been ordered to shoot on sight anyone who does not cooperate with them. I shall not be responsible for any casualties to Mukti Bahini men who may be suspected by my men to be enemy agents."

That was the last we heard of Mukti Bahini in that area. SFF local boat fleet entered Rangamati town ably led by Lt-Colonel B.K. Narayan against some opposition. We learnt later that the Mizo Commander Mr Lal Denga was staying with his family in Rangamati and had to be evacuated further South beyond *Chittagong* by the enemy before they could withdraw from *Rangamati*.

What unnerved the enemy more at Rangamati was the constant hovering of my helicopter over the town, undeterred by enemy machine-gun and rifle fire aimed at it; and several flights south-east of *Kaptai* in the area of *Dundumia* where I was concentrating a company strength to attack Kaptai area, and then proceed west for *Chittagong*. About 200 Mujeeb Bahini men were already despatched in that direction on foot earlier. This new threat in their rear unnerved the enemy and they withdrew from Rangamati leaving behind enormous stocks of new arms and ammunition as well as rations and petrol, oil and lubricants.

Move to Rangamati and Civic Reception

I ordered my Headquarters to move to *Rangamati* immediately. Sheikh Fazal-ul-Haq Moni, Sheikh Mujeeb's nephew, who had been accompanying us, left for Rangamati to arrange a proper civic reception for me. I tried to dissuade him but he said, this was politically important. On arrival at the airstrip within the town, I found thousands of civilians waiting for my arrival. Sheikh Fazal-ul-Haq Moni full of elation made a highly emotional speech in Bengali, which made the faces of the liberated people light up. I had picked up quite a bit of that sweet and melodious Bengali language. The citizens appreciated enormously the role played by India in getting their country liberated. That afternoon the principal of a local college called me for tea and narrated with tears in his eyes, how two Pak soldiers had raped his wife in his presence, after tying him up in broad daylight. He thanked God again and again for the freedom from fear he was now experiencing.

Later in the evening the local Buddhist tribesmen (Chakmas) who had so far sided with Pakistan. because their leader, Raja Tridip Roy, was still a minister in Pakistan, expressed their joy in this new freedom, in a ceremony in a Buddhist temple to which they invited me. They narrated some harrowing tales of torture and rape by Pakistani soldiers, and blamed the two sons of the local Raja for cooperating with them. Sensing that these young princes would be lynched by the local people. I ordered that they be taken in protective custody and assured their mother, the Rani, that all would be well when things settled down.

A British tea planter, Colonel Hume, who had married the local princess, approached me with the request for medical aid for his wife who was pregnant and for her to be allowed to use the car (all cars were seized for a period in the interest of security). I gladly agreed to both of his requests and our own Medical Officer assisted in the delivery of the child for which he and the Raja's family were very grateful.

Before we entered Rangamati and as I was assembling an armada of local boats to land fresh commandos in the heart of the city, where the swollen river waters would easily transport us, I received an urgent signal from the Army Chief. It said that intercepts of enemy wireless indicated they were to withdraw by sea from Dacca to Chittagong and then escape via Arakan Road into Burma. I was ordered to move a strong Commando Force to *Dohazari* area and block this Arakan Road. The Army Chief gave me two days in which to move scores of mile into an enemy infested and unreconnoitered area. He admitted it was very short notice but added:

> I know that my Fifth Army can do the Job.

We had been raised to the status of an 'Army' by our chief who now thought too much of our potential. We could not only capture Rangamati and Chittagong without air support or guns but could move like phantoms, reach *Dohazari*, blow up the bridge at that point on *River Sangu* and deny the Arakan Road to the Pak Army on the run to Burma.

I knew we were the only force in that area who could do this task but the time was too short. I had also heard that there was a possibility of the powerful US Seventh Fleet reaching the area of Cox Bazar or even further north, forming a bridgehead in this area and evacuating all the Pak troops. No unconventional Force of our size had ever been confronted with such immense odds.

We had only two helicopters (ME 4) working. The pilots were not prepared to take more than 8 commandos with their full loads of arms and ammunition. My requirement was thirteen in each craft. We dismantled all that we thought was unnecessary in the craft and loaded 13 men in each. The creaking in the body showed the strain but the engines took it. I continued to demand more helicopters which I was informed were sitting idle not very far, but they never arrived. In the place of helicopters we received a new message of congratulations from our Chief which said:

> I have implicit faith in my New Army.

This naturally made us attempt the impossible.

While we were rushing south to dominate the Arakan Road, our North column was busy destroying all remnants of the enemy posts which still held out north of *Rangamati*. We got another signal from our chief:

> You have my admiration. Well done. Keep moving fast.

Another victory by my commander in the north brought yet another congratulatory signal from the Chief:

> Well done, keep cracking. I have full confidence in you.

At this stage the first helicopter had taken off at 0550 hrs for a hill feature, ten miles to the south-east of *Dohazari* bridge, which was my important target for destruction. If we could blow up this bridge over river *Sangu*, the enemy had very little chance of escaping to Burma. My total concentration was therefore on this task. In any case the Army Chief was expecting all bridges like Dohazari bridge destroyed by first light on 12th December.

I thought it would be good for me to be with the leading Coy which was being concentrated for the task of destroying Dohazari bridge. There was no time for me to wait for an 'all clear' signal by the men who had flown in the first helicopter. I, therefore, sat in the second helicopter which took off about five minutes after the first one, to build up a platoon strength of 26 men, who were to clear the area of our landing and then move quickly in the direction of Dohazari bridge to destroy it by surprise if possible. Major S.S. Negi who later won a Vir Chakra was ordered by me on landing to push out a strong patrol to *Bindraban* which was known to have about 200 Pathans who were supported by the local Raja (the Bomong Chief) who was reported to be pro-Pakistan and lived in his palace in the town. Major Negi was also ordered to send a platoon each to river *Sangu* bend to his north-west and send another platoon towards *Dohazari* bridge and destroy it at the earliest. He was greatly helped by the Naval Air bombardment which continued along this road and even hit the bridge at one end.

This allowed our commandos to close in this bridge and kill and dislodge the Pakistani soldiers defending the bridge. Our attack so demoralised the enemy that the survivors started running back to Chittagong blowing all the bridges behind them—a task which would have taken us a big effort to achieve on our own.

The Pathans at Bindraban hastily withdrew south in local boats along *river Sangu* to *Ruma* and beyond guided by local Chakmas and Mizos. They mistook our helicopter strength and felt scores of sorties were bringing in a large number of commandos to surround *Bindraban*. In actual fact I had asked my helicopter to make sweeps over the town, river and hill area close to *Bindraban*. The Raja's palace being the biggest building there engaged my attention and I flew very close to its roof many a times to see if I could spot any unusual activity. In this very palace the Raja invited me for tea and told the amusing story of how they were all scared by the sorties over the palace, expecting everytime that a big bomb would be dropped to destroy the building.

Many Opportunities Missed

We were missing scores of excellent opportunities to take prisoners and arms for want of adequate air transport. I kept on pleading in signal after signal for at least two more helicopters, so that along with two of our own we could transport a worthwhile force in a chosen target area, but to no avail. We could not exploit the fear that we created in a sudden move into an unexpected area. At one time I sent just a section strength walking to accept the surrender of 250 Pathans who had sent a word to us, thinking we were a big force. Sometimes the hoax worked. Many times it did not.

Enemy Hopes of Escape Destroyed

After destroying the Dohazari bridge and clearing *river Sangu* in *Bindraban* area we were in a position to tell the Army Chief that the additional task of denying the Arakan Road and transportation along river *Sangu* had been accomplished well in time and that he may warn the enemy commander that the whole of this area had been developed into a death trap out of which none of them could escape. It was after this assurance of ours that the warning given by the Army Chief to the Pak General Niazi became effective and he seriously started thinking of unconditional surrender. The Special Frontier Force can rightly claim a big role in the enemy surrender.

I received the following signal from the Army Chief:

> I am proud of your achievements. My congratulations. Keep moving and the prize will be yours.

Chittagong—the Bone of Contention

Mujeeb Bahini's boys who had earlier infiltrated into Chittagong Port and City, arranged boats for my force to cross over into *Chittagong* at night. They captured the radio station where they had their sympathisers on the staff and even announced surrender by Pak troops.

Just at this time I received a signal from Army Headquarters that my force will not cross River Karnaphul and remain to the south of it. This was to deny me the opportunity of entering Chittagong which was to the north of River Karnaphuli. The signal also said that two Army brigades were on their way to accept surrender of Pak Army troops located at *Chittagong*.

It would have been perhaps too much for the Army to allow a small Guerilla Force to accept the surrender of Pak troops there and to be able to say that they captured this big port city. We were terribly disappointed and Sheikh Fazal-ul-Haq Moni did not mince words while expressing his surprise and anger at this.

CHAPTER 15

The Unconditional Surrender

Lt-General J.S. Aurora on the Indian side and Lt-General Niazi on the Pakistan side signed the Cease-fire Agreement after General Niazi agreed to the unconditional surrender of his troops at 1631 hrs on 16 December 1971. Pak troops fought well wherever they chose to fight and under extremely difficult conditions. Few could have won a war of this nature in a vicious terrain, with a totally hostile population and over a thousand miles from the main base, separated from the main theatre of operation, by a hostile country. Their fanatic zeal for proving their martial superiority clouded their vision and they could not see the hopelessness of their situation *vis-a-vis* a country five times bigger in size, nine times stronger in manpower and scores of times richer in resources.

India, though highly elated, played it deliberately on a low key. The inherent power of India had begun to show and the whole of Asia looked on in awe. The so-called friends of Pakistan began to have second thoughts on their policy. Prime Minister Indira Gandhi who had shown such statesmanship and courage was conferred the title of "Bharat Ratna" by the President on the unanimous recommendation of a jubilant and grateful Parliament. General Sam Manekshaw, the brain and inspiration behind this whole operation, became the first Field Martial of India. Simla agreement was the outcome of this war which brought a new Muslim Nation—Bangladesh—into being and destroyed the Two-nation Theory based on religion (which formed the basis of partition of the Indian subcontinent) for all times to come. India released the captured Pak territory along with the 93,000 prisoners of war, asked for no war reparations and declared a unilateral Cease-fire on the Western front.

As a result of this War India gained nothing except the goodwill of Mr Bhutto, who continued to rave against India calling for the settlement of a long settled dispute over the possession of Kashmir, and the hope that Pakistan would get over its obsession of conquering Hindu India and repeating the history of earlier Muslim invaders.

Sheikh Mujeeb, the new ruler of Bangladesh, got busy refurbishing his own image amongst his coreligionists and establishing the identity of his new nation in the world forums.

His country was in ruins, the treasury empty and problems of human misery insurmountable. The infrastructure of civil administration and the police was too disorganised and in some cases was unreliable and thus not to be of much help to him in the reconstruction of his economy and in establishing law and order. The Army was still trying to find its feet and fearful of the prospect of absorbing seniormost Bengali officers being repatriated by the Pakistan Army. The most dominant political party, the Awami League, had yet to readjust itself to its new role of a responsible ruling party in a newly independent country, whose freedom had been primarily won by the freedom fighters of all hues. Maulana Bhashani was at his old game of claiming his own pound of flesh. Leftists and marxists were exerting their own pressures quite disproportionate to their numbers and the youth clung to their weapons fearing an internal turmoil. Scarcity of necessities of life kept mounting. Prices were steadily rising along with the expectations of masses who wanted the end of this nightmare at any cost. Big-power help was available but at a heavy price.

Sheikh Mujeeb alone had the charisma to stand between stability and chaos. Mujeeb demanded discipline and hard work by the nation and time above all. But would that highly emotional and excitable nation allow him the time. This was the imponderable question. India was going all out to put the new nation back on its rails but had to contend against great forces of disruption, which looked at the latest power of India with some trepidation and hated Mujeeb's friendship with India.

New Role of the Special Frontier Force

My troops were still being fired at. There were many Mizos, Razakars, Chakmas and the stranded but armed men of the Para-Military Forces roaming the ideal Guerilla area of Chittagong Hill Tracts. I wanted to clear my position with the Army Chief on whose orders I had ordered cease-fire. I told the Chief of my dilemma and sought clarification about what to do when fired upon and what to do with the roaming gangs of Mizo desperados who obey no Pak command. He said I should only fire in self defence but ordered me to chase the Mizos out of Chittagong Hill Tracts if they were not prepared to surrender and obey their own Pak higher command. The Chief also said:

> You have a new and interesting adventure each day. Best of Luck.

When we had cleared the area and forced the Mizos to surrender to our posts along Mizoram border, the Army Chief sent me the following signal:

> Every Message you send makes fascinating reading. Delighted by your success against Mizos. Consider that you can now rest on your Laurels. Instructions for your evacuation to India follow.

The fighting did not stop. We had some more work to do against the Mizos. The Chief again encouraged us by a touching message appreciated by all ranks:

> COAS sends you strong approbation and congratulations to your Force on excellent work done. The tuffness of your task fully appreciated.

After receiving civic receptions at Rangamati, Kaptai and other towns we felt that the Bangladesh population was very grateful for the sacrifices we had made for their liberation. Sheikh Moni was approached by a delegation who wanted to honour me and my force for what we had done against such heavy odds. I thought it would be in the fitness of things, if my staff at New Delhi, who had laboured through this gruelling campaign without any publicity or approbation, was given an opportunity to attend this civic reception at *Chittagong*. They should also visit the area of our exploits and gain experience which may help them in their professional career. I wanted Mr RN Kao to come also but he has always avoided the lime light and, therefore, excused himself. He, however, very kindly agreed to my suggestion and sent Brigadier BB Bhatnagar who had been awarded an Ati Visisht Sewa Medal for his outstanding services at SFF Headquarters, Brigadier (later Lt-General) T.S. Oberoi who was responsible for the training of our Mujeeb Bahini boys and Colonel BD Kaushal responsible for administration of the Force. I included the names of Colonel Iqbal Singh, my Chief of Staff who was mentioned in despatches, Colonel Purkyastha Vr C and Lt-Colonel Khanna to accompany me during the reception.

Even here the corps Headquarters in the beginning refused to permit a reception being given to me and my Force. I was told this was done due to a pique since they wanted a reception in honour of their corps commander, whose troops had accepted the surrender of Pak troops there and the civilian leaders who were of Awami League wanted to give it to me and my force first, since they knew who had done the most work in that area. In fact, Sheikh Moni became so livid with this attitude of our Army that he said, "No reception will be given in Chittagong to any military leader and I shall see to that".

Anyhow later with some persuation the Army authorities agreed to allow this reception as a special favour to me after Brigadier Oberoi spoke to one of his senior friends in that HQ and told him about the serious political repercussions their refusal may have.

We were received on a well-decorated platform by Sheikh Fazal-ul-Haq Moni, Mr Abu Saleh MNA from that area and other leaders. They made very laudatory speeches in praise of my country and our Prime Minister. I began my speech in Bengali and was given a big applause. After the first few sentences which I could pronounee faultlessly, I continued the remainder of my speech in English, which was translated into Bengali by Mr Moni. There were endless crowds exhibiting enthusiasm which can come only on one's liberation. Hundreds of trucks and cars had arrived in this many miles long procession. I was presented with a parchment of honour along with an EPNS boat, the symbol of Awami League party, and a photograph of Sheikh Mujeebur Rehman. The parchment of honour was beautifully worded and handwritten in Bengali, showering high praise on me.

It was a memorable day for all of us. We were then entertained to music by the radio artists of Dacca.

CHAPTER 16

Strategic Concepts and the Conventional War

Surrender

Just 5 days after the declaration of War by Pakistan, the situation had started looking grim for the Pakistan Army in Bangladesh. Indian Army appeared to be closing in on Dacca. On 8th December, the UN sought the permission for safe air lifting of foreign nationals from Dacca. On 9th December the Pakistan Governor Malik and General Niazi sent simultaneous messages to Islamabed about the seriousness of the situation, and Governor Malik sought permission for immediate ceasefire and political settlement. General Yahya Khan did not hesitate to agree. Governor Malik then approached Mr Henry, the Assistant Secretary General of UN in Dacca, to arrange a cease-fire. These news naturally spread and were broadcast by several radio stations. General Manekshaw had also broadcast a Special Message to the Pakistan forces telling them that they should surrender at once if they wanted their safety. Pakistan troops and their Commanders knew at this stage that they had lost but continued to mark time awaiting official confirmation.

The coup de grace came when the Indian MIGs hit the roof of the very hall in which Governor Malik was holding a meeting of important Civil and Military officials at 11 a.m. at the Government House in Dacca. His message to Islamabad had been intercepted a short while earlier and our Air Force got the opportunity to give a proof of its precision bombing. The Governor and his advisers ran to the Air Raid Shelter and prayed. The Governor wrote his resignation in the Air Raid Shelter and moved after bombing to the security of International Red Cross at the Hotel International.

Whereas the MIGs shook the Civil officials to surrender, the Pakistani Army needed some concrete proof of the arrival of large bodies of the Indian Army into Dacca before packing their belongings. While the intrepid General Sagat was still struggling to build up his formations across river Meghna, the Mountain Gunners (the elite of the Indian Artillery) dismantled one gun of 65 Mountain Regiment and carried it forward manpack and bombarded targets in Dacca, heralding not only the arrival of 57 Inf Division on the outskirts of Dacca but the imperative need for Pakistani defenders to pack up.

Incidentally General Chowdhury (nick-named Moochoo) during the Police Action in Hyderabad, soon after partition, had used the same trick to help the fanatic Razakars (who wanted to fight to the last man—last round) make up their minds and run for life. He had used a troop of 40 Medium Regt to shell their defences before advancing the Infantry. The thud of just four 200-lb well placed shells was enough to settle the issue. After that it was plain sailing.

Since General Niazi sent his proposal of cease-fire through Mr. Spivack—the US Consul General in Dacca who relayed every message to Pakistan or India through Washington, the American military authorities knew the state of morale of the Pakistan forces and this may well have dampened their enthusiasm to speed up the 7th Fleet for their rescue.

"The Bastards Sitting in Pindi have Got US Licked" was the first remark made by Lt-General AKK Niazi to Major General Nagra, the gallant Indian General who had driven into his HQ to discuss surrender terms of Pakistan soldiers. Major General JFR Jacob, the Chief of Staff of Eastern Command, arrived soon afterwards bringing a draft of the terms of unconditional surrender by the Pakistan Army. This was followed soon afterwards by a helicopter formation carrying General Aurora and his wife, Air Marshal Dewan, Vice-Admiral Krishnan, Lt-General Sagat Singh with his Divisional Commanders. All of these were the heroes of the Bangladesh War except Mrs Aurora who was taken by General Aurora possibly to soften the shock of surrender to Niazi. The Instrument of Surrender was signed at an impressive ceremony on the afternoon of 16 December 1971 by Lt-General AKK Niazi and Lt-General Jagjit Singh Aurora. In the presence of hundreds of thousands of Bangladeshis—some still boiling with rage against their erstwhile oppressors. With this over 90,000 prisoners of war surrendered to the Indian Army and sought protection against Mukti

Bahini and others who had suffered. It is a great pity that Colonel M.A.G. Osmany, who was appointed the Chief of Mukti Bahini by the Provisional Government of Bangladesh on 13 April 1971, and who had done so much to organise Mukti Bahini was not present during this surrender ceremony to which he was entitled and Group Captain Khondkar represented the Bangladesh forces. Somebody had tripped up and missed an historic opportunity to cement bonds of comradeship with the Bangladesh army of the future.

How did all this happen?

When posted, in Shillong in Command of 22 Mountain Regt., I had an occasion to visit the border of Bangladesh (then known as East Pakistan) criss-crossed with many streams and thick with trees and haze. It gave me the impression that a few determined and well armed men could delay the advance of formations and Divisions indefinitely. Tanks would be of little use and the Air Force could give very little support in that visibility and the Field and heavy guns would get stuck in the mud with one good rain, this being a rainy area. It was an excellent Guerrila country where tough infantry men supported by Animal Pack Mountain Guns was the only possibility. In fact I had boasted and said in a conference that if I were given the task of defending that territory with one Infantry Division, I could fight any aggression indefinitely and that mechanised formations had little or no role to play in that terrain particularly in rainy season.

How is it then that over 5 Divisions of well equipped and tough Pakistani soldiers surrendered within 14 days of fighting?

Strategic Direction

India

All wars are essentially battles of minds—minds of not only the opposing Army Formation Commanders but the minds of the Civilian Political Authority that makes vital life and death decisions for the nations before, during and after the war. India was fortunate in having a highly seasoned, brave and decisive lady—Mrs Indira Gandhi as the Prime Minister. She was assisted by a dedicated politician like

Mr D.P. Dhar, as the Minister in charge of this operation; some of the ablest civil officials as Mr P.N. Haksar, and an outstanding Foreign Secretary, Mr T.N. Kaul.

External intelligence was in the efficient hands of Shri R.N. Kao, who had no equal in experience or intellect.

No country could wish for a better or more cohesive set up at the top, to conduct a war which had the threat of Super Power involvement. All these leaders appeared cool and unhurried and often gave the appearance of an academic council but nothing missed their sharp intellect. No decision, however risky, was ever delayed.

The Defence set up was equally harmonious and effective. General (now Field Marshal) SHFJ Manekshaw, M.C., with his personal charm and efficiency was loved and respected by his colleagues—Air Chief Marshal PC Lal, DFC, in the Air Force and Admiral SM Nanda in the Navy. All of them were located in Delhi and were therefore easily available for consultations. A lot has been said in favour of the Chief of Defence Staff system where all three services come under the command of one person. It has advantages as well as disadvantages and I think it is not an absolute necessity for India. Our democratic system of rotating the Chairmanship of the Chiefs of Staff Committee between the Army, Navy and Air Force Chiefs for a term engenders free discussion and voluntary cooperation and has a lot to commend itself. During this period Field Marshal Manekshaw was the Chairman and functioned admirably.

There was also close cooperation at the theatre level. Lt-General J.S. Aurora, the GOC-in-C Eastern Command—in charge of Bangladesh operations, was in touch with Air Marshal AC Dewan, PVSM, at Shillong and Vice-Admiral N Krishnan, PVSM, DSC, at Visakhapatnam after finalising plans together. Perhaps it would have been better if all three were located in one place like Calcutta but there were problems and it was thought best for the Air and Navy to move their HQ to places where they could best exercise their command. Undoubtedly Liaison Officers with rapid communication from these arms, stayed at the Eastern Command Headquarters.

Bengali Units of the erstwhile East Pakistan like the East Bengal Regiment and the East Pakistan Rifles along with Mukti Bahini volunteers were distributed under command of Army Formations deployed along the borders while their Chief, Colonel Osmany, remained in close touch with General Aurora's Headquarters, in Calcutta.

Pakistan

Pakistan had no civilian set up. General Yahya Khan was the President, the Chief Martial Law Administrator and the Chief of all Defence Forces. One cannot pity a man more than when he occupies all the seats of Power under these circumstances and particularly when he has strictly limited capabilities. Mr Z.A. Bhutto, the only political leader, had exhausted his utility by going to Dacca with General Yahya ostensibly to help resolve the political issue by a dialogue with Sheikh Mujeebur Rehman and ending up by approving the massacre of Bangladeshis by General Tikka Khan at Chittagong and saying "Thank God! Pakistan has been saved through this massacre". He was to pay the price of supporting the Pakistani Generals later. But he waited in the wings hoping to take over as the next Civilian Monarch of Pakistan as soon as circumstances became favourable. Meanwhile he headed a Pakistani delegation to Beijing on 5 November to seek their support for this war.

Military Strategy: The Pakistan strategy was based on the powerful support they expected from China and USA as a reward for their part in bringing about a rapproachment between them. Indo-Soviet Treaty of Friendship signed on 9 August 1971 effectively neutralised the new Axis of USA and China from directly influencing the impending catastrophe. But hopes of intervention by USA (or UN at their instance) persisted in Pakistan and they decided to fight a defensive battle which they had no chance of winning. Furthermore Niazi chose a technique which could not even delay defeat and allow their friends to come to their succour.

The task given to Lt-General Niazi who came on promotion, was "to prevent internal subversion and defend Pakistan against external aggression." The first part of preventing internal subversion cannot be undertaken by a regular soldier, particularly when the whole population is seething with discontent and harbours nothing but hatred for the occupying forces of a different race.

The task of 'Defence against external aggression' was not clearly defined in either political or military terms. No written directive or instruction was given to General Niazi nor was he briefed by anyone. It is indeed amazing that General Niazi in his enthusiasm to prove his courage under such overwhelming conditions, did not insist on a written brief or instruction. No Military Commander at that level would move without one.

Although it should have been clear to General Niazi as daylight when he took over in September 1971, that the Indian Army stood poised and ready along his North, East and Western borders to launch an all out offensive, he persuaded himself to believe that the only aim of the Indian Army was to secure a large enough base within East Pakistan where they could transfer the Pakistani refugees and instal an *ad hoc* Bangladesh Government. He, therefore, decided to deny this objective to the enemy and undertook the total defence of every inch of the territory under his charge. He particularly wanted to deny the important towns to the Indian Army which could make political headlines. He, therefore, disposed of his troops in order to fight major battles along the borders up to the river lines of Ganga, Jamuna, Brahmaputra and Meghna. Towns lend themselves excellently to Defence and become famous "landmarks of history" like the Defence of Stalingrad. He, therefore, chose towns like Chittagong, Comilla, Bhairab Bazar, Sylhet, Mymensingh, Jamalpur, Rangpur, Bogra, Jhenida and Jessore which dominated the roads along the borders and ordered them to be made into impregnable fortresses to be defended to the last man and last round.

General Niazi's plans had been accepted by the Pak Army Headquarters. General Hamid, the C-in-C Pakistan Army, had visited him in September, soon after his take over and discussed his plans with him. He had, however, said that Dacca should be treated as crucial for the defence of East Pakistan which is obvious. I am sure Niazi was conscious of it and had plans for his troops to fall back for the defence of Dacca but he never gave an inkling of this to any of his subordinate commanders lest it affects their morale and they start withdrawing prematurely. There was no reason, however, why he could not have made preparations for the defence of Dacca with remnants of his 36 Infantry Division which had been assigned this responsibility as well as other formations close to Dacca.

Niazi was right in assessing that these towns would be the first objectives given to the Indian Army formations but he was wrong to think that Indian Army would never bypass them and proceed to the very heart of the battlefield—*Dacca.*

Pakistani troop dispositions were as follows:

- ***North-West Sector:*** The most important sector with the Siliguri corridor—the bottleneck which connects the eastern regions with the rest of India and which is within easy reach of the Chinese bases in Chumbi valley. This sector also offered another bottleneck at *Hilli-Gaibanda* further south, which can seal all Pakistani forces in the south and fulfil all the conditions of a limited offensive which India was expected to take. Major General Nazar Hussain Shah, GOC 16 Infantry Division, was assigned the defence of this sector and was allotted 10 Infantry battallions, one Mujahid battalion and one Regiment of Chaffee tanks.
- ***South-West Sector:*** Closest to Calcutta with the old route to Dacca via Goalundo Ghat ferry passing through it. It also had the port of Chalna besides the important towns of Jessore and Khulna. This was to be defended by Major General MH Ansari's Division with 8 Infantry battalions and one squadron of Chaffee tanks.
- ***Central Sector:*** Tangail and Dacca were the places of importance in this Sector which is surrounded on all sides by rivers and has very poor communications. This was allotted for defence to Major General Jamshed Khan, GOC 36 Infantry Division. Only two Infantry battalions with one Mortar battery were allotted to him. He was given no armour.
- ***Eastern Sector:*** This was the nearest approach to Dacca. Sylhet in the north provided good scope for Mukti Bahini operations and Chittagong in the south, the only port which could be used for reinforcement and rescue operations, was considered indefensible. General Niazi assigned two Divisions to this Sector with 14 Infantry battalions and one squadron of Armour. One brigade group was assigned the task of defending the indefensible Chittagong. This southern portion was later reinforced in November when Niazı felt the main Indian thrust was coming from this direction. Besides, regular troops, large numbers of

> Chinese trained Mizos and Para-Military Forces from Pakistan were deployed in the Chittagong Hill Tracts not only for the safety of the port but to keep the Arakan Road leading into Burma from Chittagong open for final withdrawal, if necessary. Lal Denga—the Mizo National Front leader had his headquarters in Rangamati in Chittagong Hill Tracts and Pak Para-Military Forces spread along the hills right up to Cox's Bazar.

This is how the Pakistan Army deployed itself irretrievably for destruction, subordinating Military necessity to political desirability. The time chosen to declare War along with the bombing of Indian cities was not during the monsoon when the Indian Army would have got stuck in the mud and stranded across flooded rivers with no road communication functioning, but on 3 December 1971 when the mechanised Indian Army could have a free run of the land and would be fully prepared to do so and when the passes in the north would be closed due to snowfall and the Chinese in no position to assist Pakistan even if they so willed.

Vinashkale Viparit Buddhi

(At the time of destruction, the intellect forsakes one.)

Early April 1971 had been suggested by some military strategists as the best period for Indian offensive when East Pakistan had just about one Division strength, passes in the north were still closed due to snow and the Indian Army had enough troops in the vicinity to attack. Air and Navy would have carried out their roles as effectively as they did in December. I feel it would not have been as spectacular a victory if at all and our offensive may even have failed for lack of sufficient planning and preparations. One should give full credit to Field Marshal Manekshaw for undertaking operations after thorough preparations. Had he succumbed to public opinion or political pressure, he would not have acquired the stature he did as a result of his outstanding victory.

Planning at Eastern Command Headquarters was most meticulous. It could not be otherwise since Lt-General JFR Jacob, the Chief of Staff, is an efficient officer. General Aurora's forte has also been in planning and training of which he has had considerable experience in service.

There is some substance in the criticism that the planning was not bold enough. Plan can be as bold as the Commanders and troops entrusted to execute it and the availability of implements with which the aims can be accomplished. General Lachhman Singh, an eminent Commander in this war, has commented in his excellent book *Victory in Bangladesh* about there being no mention of the capture of Dacca in the orders issued to the Indian Army and therefore lack of adequate planning for crossing the river obstacles to reach Dacca or vertical envelopment of Dacca with the help of helicopters.

We have no helicopter fleet at our disposal and the limited number of ME-4 helicopters we have are not an integral part of the Army for training and use. Primarily they are used for administration and casualty evacuation and are in the charge of the Air Force. This is a serious lacuna in modern warfare and should be set right as early as possible. But in 1971 no attempt was made by the Army to ask for them as an essential requisite for war nor was any training carried out in this direction. We were fortunate in having General Sagat Singh and General Gonsalves who are paratroopers and who did make excellent use of the few helicopters that were allotted to them for crossing river Meghna and reaching Dacca. In fact General Sagat never allowed any helicopter allotted to him out of his sight and waited breathlessly for the opportunity to use them for this very purpose. My own complaint against General Sagat not releasing even one helicopter for my Special Frontier Force fighting valiantly at his flanks is based on this very premise.

With regard to General Lachman's complaint that Dacca was not mentioned as an objective either by the Army or Command Headquarters. I would say that although Dacca was the political heart of Bangladesh it was not the military citadel of East Pakistan. The task given to the Eastern Command was "to destroy the bulk of Pakistan forces in East Pakistan." Once that was achieved Dacca was merely a walkover to hoist the Bangladesh Flag. Incidentally 4 Corps did go for Dacca at the right time after the Pakistan troops had been defeated in detail. Often enough the Senior Commanders while launching the first phase of as large an operation as that of Bangladesh, decide on the final objective which may change as a result of Phase I, or other unforeseen circumstances but the alternative plans for likely final objectives are always well thought out by the theatre Commanders in consultation with the political authority. There was no excuse, however, for making no preparations for quick river crossing by troops particularly those closest to Dacca nor was there any excuse for not making provision for vertical envelopment plan for Dacca much earlier. It was indeed a surprise for me to know that ready-made plan were handed over to formations to execute and the normal drill of lower formations making their own plans which are coordinated at higher levels was not done. There was plenty of time for it and it would definitely have been better to get those responsible for fighting involved in planning earlier. Be that as it may, the Indian Army was disposed as follcws:

- ***North-West Sector:*** Lt-General M.L. Thapar, GOC 33 Corps, the only General Officer in the Eastern theatre who had commanded a Division in battle earlier, was allotted the task of cutting the Waistline at Hilli-Gaibanda and capture Bogra in the south and Rangpur in the north. He was allotted besides 20 Mountain Division, one additional Infantry Battalion and two Armoured Regiments less one Squadron and one Engineer Brigade. The 71 Mountain Brigade was to operate from the North in addition.

  This was strategically the most important Sector and therefore both the strength of the enemy as well as his resistance along well prepared defences was the heaviest. The main oflensive in this Sector was undertaken by 20 Mountain Division under Maj General Lachhman Singh, Vr C, who gave a splendid showing by his use of armour and improvisation. Unfortunately, a direct assault was ordered on the prepared defences of Hilli against the advice of the Corps and Div Command by General Aurora himself who restricted the assaulting troops to one battalion and did not allow use of Armour. This and some other attacks launched frontally against Hilli failed as they should have and resulted in heavy casualties. Later the plans were revised by the Command Headquarters at the instance of the local Commanders. It was one of the toughest battles and lasted from 23 November to the day of surrender.

- ***South-West Sector:*** The Sector closest to Calcutta was given to recently promoted Lt-General TN Raina. MVC, of 2 Corps, a veteran of the 1962 Chinese War who later became the Chief of

Staff of the Indian Army. The Corps Headquarters was raised in October to control two Divisions, one Parachute Brigade less one Battalion, one Armoured Regiment plus one Squadron. Their task was to capture Jessore and Khulna-Chalna. Eastern Command had rightly given time bound objectives to various formations in this Corps with their eye on Dacca. The 4 Mountain Division (Red Eagle) commanded by Maj General M.S. Brar took Jhenida Sector and Maj General Dalbir Singh, GOC 9 Infantry Division, took Jessore Sector after very tough battles.

- ***Central Sector:*** This Sector was closest to Dacca and yet given the last priority by both adversaries.

  This Sector had the unique distinction of having *Tiger Siddiqui*, a Bengali Guerilla leader, defying the armed might of Pakistan forces and keeping his Tangail area free of enemy troops. This patriot joined the advancing Indian Army and cooperated freely with them. I had the privilege to meet him at Dacca soon after the surrender by Pakistan Army.

  Maj General Gurbux Singh Gill of 101 Communication Zone was given the task of clearing this area under the direct Command of General Aurora. He had 95 Mountain Brigade under Brig HS Khar and FT Sector under Brig Sant Singh along with one Mountain Regiment, two Batteries of heavy mortars and one Field Coy Engineers. General Gill was seriously wounded by a mine explosion and was replaced by Maj General GC Nagra who asked for reinforcements to reach Dacca sooner but was rebuffed. Pakistanis fought well at Jamalpur under Sultan Ahmad, a gallant officer. General Nagra rushed forward from the North towards Dacca. Pakistani troops had lost morale on seeing a para-drop of Indian troops in Tangail area which was already a free domain under Siddiqui.

- ***Eastern Sector:*** This Sector which was closest to Dacca had Lt-General Sagat Singh in Command of 4 Corps who knew when to act boldly. This Corps was allotted 3 Divisions less one Brigade (57 Mountain Div, 23 Mountain Div and 8 Mountain Div less one Brigade).

- ***Kilo Sector*** was allotted seven East Bengal Regt Battalions, Para-Military Forces and Mukti Bahini.

The task of clearing *Sylhet Sector* was given to Maj General Krishna Rao, GOC 8 Mountain Div, who was controlling Nagaland with six Infantry Brigades earlier. He has been the Chief of Army Staff with a lot of experience behind him.

This Sector saw many innovations, General Sagat decided to heli-lift 4/5 Gorkha Rifles close to Sylhet. Nine MI-4S were provided to concentrate more than a Company strength in 1½ hours. Later two Mountain guns were also heli-lifted but the enemy made it impossible to land more troops by helicopters. Sylhet surrendered to Krishna Rao on early morning of 16 December.

- ***Bhairab Bazar Sector:*** Maj General BF Gonsalves after capturing Akhaura consulted his equally audacious Corps Comdr Sagat and changed direction from the original plan sent by Command Headquarters to go for Brahmanbaria instead of Daudkandi and thus reached closer to Meghna and Dacca. The Artillery was left behind and so were many other essential details that could not keep pace.

  Soon after General Sagat decided that the enemy was totally disorganised and this called for crossing of Meghna by a heli-lift and closing in on Dacca. Both Sagat and Gonsalves agreed to contain and bypass Brahmanbaria and cross Meghna to reach Dacca for quick results.

  This is where the initiative and boldness of local Commanders brought victory so early within our reach. *Narsingdi* area which was out of the range of enemy artillery fire and not connected by a road for quick Pak advance was chosen as the bridgehead across Meghna. General Gonsalves, air observation post officer of repute, and an experienced paratrooper was to command the troops of 57 Division leading this advance. Group Captain Chandan Singh known for his courage was to assist this air-borne operation. It was a successful operation and turned the tide of war. I am inclined to believe that the teaming of officers like Sagat-Gonsalves and Chandan was planned and not an accident.

- ***Chandpur Sector:*** This was allotted to Maj General R.B. Hira, MVC, GOC 23 Infantry Div, with the task of clearing Commilla, Laksham and Chandpur.

Containing and bypassing strong enemy positions our troops reached Chandpur which had been vacated on 9 December. Mynamati surrendered to 181 Brigade on 16 December morning and 4 Corps troops entered Chittagong on 17 December after the announcement of surrender without any fighting.

- ***Chittagong:*** The importance of Chittagong in this War cannot be over-emphasised. It was not only the heart centre of the most difficult terrain in Bangladesh, but also the main port of reinforcement for Pakistan force—their life line. It also dominated and controlled the only land-route of withdrawal for Pak troops—the Arakan Road which enters Burma near Cox's Bazar. This was an ideal area where well stocked Pak troops and Para-Military Forces could fight almost indefinitely, if they decided to make a stand and could even be picked up by the American 7th Fleet which was only 100 km from Chittagong at the time of surrender. This vital area was entrusted to the Special Frontier Force of hill-men Guerillas under the Command of Maj General S.S. Uban who also controlled the functioning of the Mujeeb Bahini throughout Bangladesh from his Headquarters in Chittagong Hill Tracts.

  Chittagong was the main objective for 4 Corps. General Uban pleaded with Field Marshal Manekshaw that the task of capturing Chittagong should be entrusted to his unconventional force. He could not convince Manekshaw that almost a battalion strength of Guerillas without Mortar, Artillery or Air support and without any means of crossing rivers could capture that objective. Uban then tried to convince the Minister D.P. Dhar who was thrilled with the prospect of a Guerilla Force taking on such a difficult task. Dhar promised to persuade Manekshaw. Extraordinary successes of the Special Frontier Force in Chittagong Hill Tracts later, however, induced the Army Chief to reevaluate the potential of this Force which he now termed his "Army of the East" and to which he offered this rich prize Chittagong as their objective. This book narrates the reasons why.

CHAPTER 17

Visit to Dacca

Bangladesh was now free. The Provisional Government had started working as a full-fledged Government in Dacca, under the Prime Ministership of that dedicated leader Tajuddin. Sheikh Moni suggested that I should visit Dacca to meet those hundreds of Mujeeb Bahini boys we had infiltrated earlier and who had made immense sacrifices to lower the morale of the Pakistani occupation Army. He wanted me to meet Begum Mujeeb who had recently been released from Pakistani custody under dramatic circumstances by an Indian Major. He also wanted to guage the political climate in Dacca. Sheikh Mujeeb had still not been set free by Bhutto and Moni was not sure whether he would ever do that.

Anyway as I was getting into my helicopter I saw Moni escorting a young man to my aircraft who was so badly limping that he had to be supported on his feet by two other young men—one on either side. I recognised him; he had been trained by us in Guerilla warfare, had infiltrated into Bangladesh, was captured and tortured with electric shocks. They had failed to extract any information from him. He was now being taken to the hospital in Dacca for treatment. This youngman was all smiles when he came closer and tried to touch my feet—a common salutation amongst all Bengalis for their elders. I embraced him and said, "You are a tiger." He said, "Sir you inspired me during my training under you." We took this boy with us and reached Dacca Airport, where thousands of young Mujeeb Bahini boys and their relations and friends, unknown to me, had assembled to greet me into a free Dacca.

The whole airfield appeared to be full of people. I was mobbed. Many shook my hands. Some embraced me and got themselves photographed with me.

When I reached the Hotel International, I discovered that DP Dhar, General Manekshaw, Mr Kao and many other dignitaries had already arrived and were staying in the Hotel. The Army Chief was giving a luncheon to all the Field Commanders who had been invited for some conference but I was not invited for this meeting being an unconventional soldier. Later when they saw me arrive, last minute invitation was issued for lunch and I was allotted a place at the formal luncheon table. Army Generals as usual were full of themselves and the vital roles each had played in the victory. They behaved as if they had never heard of me or the fighting in Chittagong Hill Tracts about which only the Army Chief, General Aurora and the Corps HQ knew. I do not blame them. It was an unparalleled victory and many heads were turned.

I went to meet the Army Chief who was sitting with Mr D.P. Dhar and Mr Kao. The Army Chief and Mr Dhar congratulated me profusely and Mr Kao could not resist the temptation of embracing me to show his appreciation of all that I had achieved. SFF had brought the highest credit to him personally. He said, "I know it is not done (meaning a senior civilian embracing an Army General) but I cannot help show my admiration in this manner."

I apologised to Mr DP Dhar and those present for my coming to Dacca unannounced. Mr Dhar showed me the local English dailies which carried my full-size photograph on their first pages and talked about the tumultuous reception I had at Dacca airport. He said, "the whole world knows that the top Guerilla leader has arrived in Dacca. When we came, nobody took the slightest notice of us. Even the Army Chief was not given red carpet treatment which you have got. You have won the hearts of the revolutionary youths of Bangladesh."

I listened to this eulogy in silence. Then he took me aside and asked me if I could induce one of my foursome (Moni, Tuffail, Razak, Shiraz) to accept a ministership in the newly formed Bangladesh Cabinet. I promised to try.

All the four leaders accompanied me to Sheikh Mujeeb's house, which had now become a place of pilgrimage and Begum Mujeeb (affectionately called Bhabhi by all) was very much in demand to decide various matters. I had a cup of tea with the Begum, and met Russel—the youngest son of Sheikh Mujeeb. Jamal, the second son of the Sheikh, who had stayed with me during the difficult days and had been trained in Guerilla warfare by us, had talked so much about me and my family to his mother that I was treated as a member of the family. Kamal the eldest son who had promised me a holiday in Rangamati after the liberation of Bangladesh, was now asked by me in turn, if he would like a holiday in *Rangamati*, which was still my Headquarters. We spent some pleasant moments together. But there was still the uncertainty of Sheikh Mujeeb's return alive from Pak custody.

In consultation with Begum Mujeeb the foursome decided not to participate in the Government till Mujeeb returned and if he did not return then to chalk out their new course. Mr DP Dhar was highly disappointed when I told him the result of my talk with these youth leaders.

The new Bangladesh Government ordered withdrawal of all weapons from unauthorised people. But the first ones who were forced to give up their weapons were the Mujeeb Bahini boys and Moni was very sore about it.

He complained to me in no uncertain terms about the policy adopted by Tajuddin which according to him was to remain in power and build up the leftist forces. He even showed me some armed communist youth who were roaming in the corridors of *Intercontinental Hotel* with black cloth bands tied around their heads.

On this question of arms I was a witness to a very tough exchange of words between Mr Dhar and Moni. The latter told Mr Dhar that they would never give up arms till Sheikh's arrival in Dacca and if necessary would wage a civil war. The courage shown by Moni at this time was indeed commendable. Mr Dhar was visibly upset. Moni told me later that he had confirmed his earlier views that Mr Dhar was the worst enemy of his country. This was to have repercussion on the relationship between India and Bangladesh later. It is well known that after Sheikh Mujeeb took over, Mr DP Dhar had become a persona-non-grata, with his Government. At one stage Bangladesh refused to receive him as a representative of the Government of India. Mrs Gandhi was able to smoothen matters, since the Sheikh was greatly beholden to her for what she had done for Bangladesh.

All in all I found the atmosphere very gloomy in Dacca in the absence of Sheikh Mujeeb. The Government appeared to lack the requisite authority or lustre which is usually exhibited by popular mass leaders. Mujeeb appeared to be the soul without which the body had no value. I returned to *Rangamati* with a heavy heart. Is all the sacrifice we had made going to be futile without Mujeeb and what chances were there for Mujeeb to return to his country and power?

I went to attend a reception at Bindraban by the Raja (the *Bomong* Chief) who till late had been our enemy and was hosting Pathans and *Mizos*. He came to the airstrip with his brother to receive me and brought a shawl as a present, which I handed over to a poor man on the spot. He gave us tea and many assurances of loyalty to the new Nation. He also sent his sword to me through Colonel Purkyastha as a sign of surrender, which I sent to Sheikh Mujeeb with a recommendation that the Raja be shown leniency for his earlier support to Pak authority.

I flew to Cox's Bazar on hearing the news that about 400 Burmese Dacoits had arrived in the adjacent hills and that some Razakars from Bangladesh had joined hands with them. The Burmese brigade were reported to be sealing their borders against the entry of these undesirable elements. Awami League representatives at Cox's Bazar appeared very perturbed. I could have dealt with this new menace but we were being withdrawn to be moved out to India.

There was a reception at Kaptai which I had to attend. Prof Nurul Islam Chaudhary, Chairman of the Zonal Council, Mr Sultan Ahmad and others received us and we saw a cultural show laid on by the Collector in our honour. This was all on the 31st of December 1971–the New Year's eve. I sent New Year greeting cards to all my friends in India and sent what I thought was a beautifully worded one to the Prime Minister.

On the 1st January I sent in a further list of officers recommended for gallantry awards. Ultimately we got six Vir Chakras for Colonel PC Purkyastha, Major RK Malhotra, Major SC Sharma, Major SS Negi ACC, GB Valankar and Flight Lieutenant, Jamasji who had done exceedingly well. Five Visisht Sewa Medals were awarded including one to Major PC Mehta, our famous surgeon, who did a lot to popularise the compassion of armed forces of India towards their ailing brothers and sisters of Bangladesh one VSM was awarded to Colonel KL Vasudeva for his excellent coordination work with the Army along the borders. Five Sena Medals and eleven Mention in Despatches were also awarded, making a total of 29 awards including a Param Visisht Sewa Medal to myself and Ati Visisht Sewa Medal to Brigadier BB Bhatnagar, I was glad about Major ML Dutta, Commander of Signals, being awarded a Visisht Sewa Medal for maintaining wireless communication under most difficult circumstances. I was sorry that Assistant Coy Commander TS Bawa missed a decoration because he was recommended late and I think we had run out of our Quota. He fought very bravely and acts of his courage came to light later.

I cannot refrain from mentioning my civilian Personal Assistant Mr SD Candrolli, who acted always above and beyond the call of his duty. An exceptionally outstanding stenographer who showed courage under most difficult circumstances. How I wish I could demonstrate my appreciation of his excellent work by adding a Visisht Sewa Medal to his name. A citation in this book is the least I can do for him.

Move to Command Headquarters, Calcutta

It was necessary to tie up the details of SFF move back into India with the Command Headquarters at Calcutta. I flew to Calcutta on 2 January 1972, met my old friend General Jacob there who was the able Chief of Staff of General Aurora and fixed the details of our move back after exchanging some information with him.

I learnt that my spiritual preceptor Baba Onkarnath (a very famous Bengali Saint) had just undergone an eye operation and was in Calcutta. I went to pay my respects to him and took Sheikh Moni (Mujeeb's nephew) with me. Baba had his eyes bandaged and was lying down but he was delighted to hear of my arrival. The first question he asked me was about the condition in Bangladesh after our victory. I said, "the whole thing is going to pieces without Mujeeb who is still detained in Pakistan." I then introduced Moni to him.

Baba folded his hands and said, "Mother dear (addressing God) Mujeeb is the soul of Bangladesh. When you have done so much for that country please get Mujeeb also released at once". Then turning round to Moni, Baba said, "Do not worry. Mujeeb will come and all will be well." Baba gave a shawl to Moni as a gift with this blessing. Moni was over-whelmed and had tears in his eyes. I was certain now that all would be well.

That very afternoon as we were listening to the radio, we heard that Bhutto had publicly stated that he was going to release Mujeeb unconditionally. Under such circumstances even the atheists resume faith in God. Moni particularly remarked about Baba's prediction in the morning and its fullfilment the same day. He wanted to go and meet Baba with some fruits and flowers next morning before we left for Dacca. We were fortunate to meet Baba again and receive his blessings.

On 5 January 1972 I met Mr Tajuddin, the Prime Minister of Bangladesh, and Syed Nazrul Islam, the President. The latter was keen to have himself photographed with me because of our old association in Calcutta but the photographer took a long time coming and I had to fly back to Rangamati to arrange for our move back. We were handing over the charge to Lt-Colonel Chopra of the Dogra Regiment. North and the South columns were closed in and despatched to Chittagong to get into the ship *Vishva Vijay* which was to take all my troops to Calcutta.

I learnt that Sheikh was on his way to Dacca as the President and the father of the new Nation. He was received in Delhi by Mrs Gandhi, who herself raised slogans in his honour and captured his heart as the greatest friend he had ever had.

Colonel JA Hume, Secretary, Tea Association, Chittagong, came to thank me for all the help we had given to his princess wife during the difficult days of war. Raj Mata came to meet me and ask me if I could speak to Sheikh Mujeeb regarding her sons still in custody. I promised to do the needful and this I did.

I Meet the Sheikh

The long-awaited day arrived. I was in Dacca and the time for my meeting the Sheikh had been fixed through the agency of my friends—the youth leaders. Immediately on arrival in his house I was ushered in into his room where he stood up and took me in his embrace, saying, "You are my brother—my real brother. I cannot forget what you have done for my nation, my friends and my family. Do not ever be formal with me. Treat my house as your own.

"I know how you have staked your own life many a time to help us. I shall never forget that...." so on and so forth.

Hundreds of people were milling around his house just to see him and feel gratified. He has a charismatic personality. He was emotional and got easily carried away. He gave decisions at the spur of the moment, without giving much thought and had started behaving like an autocrat already. But he alone could deliver the goods. There was much rejoicing on his return to Dacca. Millions came to receive him at the airport and then stayed back in Dacca to enjoy the independence under Mujeeb. Expectations ran high and common people felt that their economic problems would be solved as if by a magic wand. Poor people throughout the world are like that. Trusting, adoring, honestly labouring and always hoping for better days which never come. Bengalis have an additional quality—a total lack of patience and highly excitable temperaments.

This war had left Bangladesh in ruins. All its industry, communications and other assets had been destroyed. With the best will in the world it would take a decade to put the economy of Bangladesh on an even keel.

One can only pray for a man who assumes power under such circumstances in a country populated by as inflammable a material as the Bengali race.

I came out of Mujeeb's house elated at the reception and the thought that God had made it possible for me to see the happy culmination of my mission in the historic war of liberation of Bangladesh.

I sent a big plane (AN 12) load of captured arms and ammunition to be deposited with the Army authorities.

Before I left for India, my friends, the youth leaders, came to bid me farewell. We had sworn friendship for all times to come and our common success had made the bonds even more firm. I had developed a great love for the soil of that country and great admiration for the brave men and women who constituted that nation.

When my plane landed at Palam I noticed a gathering of people with garlands of flowers and could not make out whom they had come to receive. As it turned out that was my staff who had earlier sent me a fine signal of congratulation and had now come to receive me at the Airport. Formalities over, I rushed to my house to meet my wife and children who had been anxiously awaiting my return. It was a very happy reunion. My brave and young engineer son, Jagdip Singh Uban (later Flight Leiutenant in the Indian Air Force) was extremely happy to see me and seemed proud of my achievements. Alas! He died in an air crash on duty so suddenly and so young that he left a deep void, never to be filled up, in our lives. He had proudly displayed to me the para wings he had earned after completing his jumps in his squadron. He enriched our martial traditions and left the fragrance of his sweet memory behind. May God bless his soul. He felt even more proud of me when he saw the letter written to me by the Air Chief Marshal PC Lal DFC. This letter said *inter alia.*

> ***My dear Uban***
>
> *… Though a detailed account of your activities may never be published, I know that your Force played a major part in bringing about a quick victory in the East.…*
>
> ***PC Lal***

CHAPTER 18

Sheikh Mujeeb Sends for Me

One day Mr. P.N. Haksar, the Principal Secretary of the Prime Minister, sent a message to me that on the request of Sheikh Mujeebur Rehman, the Prime Minister had agreed to my going to Dacca as Personal Adviser to the Sheikh and that I should proceed forthwith.

It was a matter of great honour for me to be sent for by name, as the adviser to Sheikh Mujeeb, who made the biggest news at that time in the whole world. On arrival in Dacca I was received at the airport by Mr. Samad, the Sheikh's Foreign Minister, who insisted on giving me a cup of tea at the airport before sending me to the city.

Sheikh Sahib received me very well and said I should stay at his official residence which I politely declined. He had no vacant room in his own house otherwise I have no doubt he would have liked me to stay with the whole family, all of whom by now knew me very well.

This time I noticed he had no security arrangements at his residence. All kinds of people were coming in and seeking interviews at unearthly hours with the Prime Minister. When I pointed this lack of proper scrutiny of people who came to meet him he said, "I am the father of the nation. Everyone has a right to approach me at any hour of the day or night. If, anyone is in distress, I cannot close my doors to him." I told him that though I admired his sentiments, he owed it to his nation to ensure his personal safety. Mr. Tuffail who was now Sheikh's Political Secretary also felt helpless in this case. I suppose popular democratic leaders have to take risks, but few go to the extent Mujeeb did.

I was put up in the famous industrialist Adamji's house and good arrangements were made for providing me with vegetarian meals.

Mujeeb was worried about three things at that time. One was the non-surrender of arms by certain groups of people, who could use them against the Government when they found an opportunity. Lots of arms caches were made during the Bangladesh war by some of the so-called freedom fighters and he was aware of that.

Second was the question of smuggling from across our common borders which could ruin his economy.

The third was the question of rehabilitation of genuine youth cadres of his country who had been trained and equipped very well by the Indian authorities and who were all unemployed. His small Army had no capacity to absorb such numbers. He just did not know how best to use them.

The Sheikh had been toying with the idea of raising a Force, which would absorb all patriotic youth of Mukti and Mujeeb Bahinis and help reconstruct the shattered economy of that nation as well as establish law and order. He wanted this force to unearth all the arms caches within the country and bring to book all elements working against the national policies. He expected to use them for anti-smuggling operations across the vast Indo-Bangladesh borders, but ultimately for reconstruction purposes in the agricultural and other fields.

I had been harping on this very theme during the training of these cadres and impressing upon them the vital necessity of reconstruction work by all partriotic youth after their country was liberated. This idea had appealed to the youth and leaders like Shiraz gave great importance to it. Many of them must have discussed this idea with the Sheikh who had got convinced that a Force of this nature would greatly help bring about stability in Bangladesh.

He discussed this idea with me and finding me in agreement issued orders for this force, which he named Jatiya Rakhkhy Bahini (JRB or National Security Force) to be raised initially with a strength of 12,000 officers and men. In order to make the best use of it, he kept it under his own command and garrisoned it at Dacca. He selected Colonel Nuruzaman, an extremely efficient officer, to command the Force and requested me to do all I could to help organise, train and equip this Force.

It took me some time to convince the Indian authorities about our role in training and equipping this Force, after the war of liberation was over. Fortunately my Government agreed to this request of the

Bangladesh Government and leaders of this Force were trained in our establishment.

This force played an important role in the formative period after independence of this nation and won the confidence of the people of Bangladesh whom it served. The newspaper reports had nothing but high praise for their incorruptible character and patriotic fervour. Even the worst enemies of the Sheikh never criticised him for this move of his at this juncture.

It is a great pity that even the most profoundly beneficial moves in the interest of that nation by the Sheikh became suspect after his massacre. Jatiya Rakhkhy Bahini (JRB) met a similiar fate to the great misfortune of Bangladesh. Anyone who knows Bengalis will vouch for their independent and fearless character. Their patriotic and national sense is also well known. JRB would have played an equally useful role in any new set up since their loyalties were basically to their nation, for the peace and prosperity of which they were prepared to sacrifice even their lives.

Mrs Gandhi visits Dacca

Sheikh Mujeeb appeared quite worried about the security of Mrs Gandhi who was visiting Dacca soon after the liberation. Law and order had not yet been established satisfactorily. All kinds of people possessed modern weapons with killing power. The police had no prestige in that country having been associated with the Pakistan authorities. Army was not fully organised. He hesitated somewhat to broach this subject to me. His mere presence along with Mrs Gandhi on the rostrum was not enough to guarantee security for as important a visitor as Mrs Gandhi. He said, "Why don't you take charge of this part, I would give you any number of men you want including men from Jatiya Rakhkhy Bahini (JRB) who adore you." I said, "I was the least competent person for this kind of job in a foreign country." He said, "I do not want any incident to take place in Dacca which may cloud our relations in the future. Anyway I shall ensure her security by various means and put some Jatiya Rakhkhy Bahini patriots also spread out amongst the masses that would assemble to welcome her and listen to her." I said, "That would be fine."

A few days later I was fortunate enough to witness a spectacle which one can never forget. A high rostrum in the shape of a boat had been constructed in the middle of a maidan for this occasion. Millions of people applauded the arrival on the rostrum of two of the most charismatic leaders in Asia—each a beloved of its own nation, but on this occasion they appeared as two formidable pillars of a new phenomenon in South Asia. The ovation was heart warming. Millions shouted "Jai Bangla", Jai Bangabandhu and Jai Indira Gandhi". People were delirious with joy when Mrs Gandhi started her speech with a few sentences of Bengali which she had learnt at Vishva-Bharati University of Tagore. To the masses it demonstrated the kinship Bangladesh had with India. No Pakistani had ever addressed them like that, in their own language of which they were so proud.

The audience was well managed by the Awami League volunteers and others. Securitymen were able to catch about seven men in different places who were carrying grenades in their pockets and behaved in an abnormal fashion.

Soon after this Mrs Gandhi and the Sheikh went towards the enclosure where the leaders of Awami League were waiting to receive them, the Sheikh started introducing these leaders to her and noticed me standing close by. He beckoned me to come nearer and taking me by the hand introduced me to Mrs Gandhi saying, "Here is your General Uban."

I folded my hands to say Namaste. I had never met her before this. She responded with a smile and then walked off with her usual grace.

Bangladesh had gone all out to show its sincerest regard for India. It looked at that time as though one of the two brothers (Bangladesh) who had parted company in a huff with the elder brother (India) in 1947, had, returned home a major, self willed and Independent but nostalgic about old family ties and full of understanding and love.

Soon afterwards Sheikh Mujeeb asked for the Indian Army to be withdrawn from Bangladesh and India started withdrawing at once. I think it was a very wise decision to withdraw the Indian Army. Had it stayed longer it would have created an impression both within and outside Bangladesh of being an occupation Army. Army in peace could only be of a nuisance value. Its prompt withdrawal was welcomed by most people throughout the world as a proof of our basically non-aggressive and peace-loving nature.

After the Army had gone, I found myself as the only Sikh moving in official circles. Many people knew me as an Indian Army General. My greatest desire was to ensure stability in that highly emotional country which had been thoroughly devastated in war.

I had done my duty to my country in befriending Bangladesh. Mujeeb had asked for me in preference to all other Generals of the Indian Army because he had a lot of confidence in my integrity and sincerity as well as my unconventional expertise.

I was conscious of the immense faith my civilian superiors had in me. I had been given no briefing either by the External Affairs Ministry or my own secretary, thus laying a very heavy responsibility on my shoulders about my role as adviser to Sheikh Mujeebur Rehman. I set the following guidelines to help me discharge my functions as adviser to the Sheikh:

(a) To achieve perfect understanding between India and Bangladesh, so that we could build our future relations on mutual trust. Essentially this was the job of the High Commissioner for India in Dacca who was a most a capable man with the additional advantage of not only the knowledge of Bengali language but also of having been born in Bangladesh.

I could only assist in the process in my own military field or in any other, in which the Sheikh sought my advice.

(b) I must do everything possible to promote the interests of Bangladesh and to bring about unity in the Armed Forces in Bangladesh who had their loyalties severely shaken during the recent war and to win over their goodwill for India. Only a solidly united Army which is loyal to Bangladesh and its elected leaders could bring about stability.

(c) To advocate a policy of forgive and forget. Pakistan had suffered a defeat from which it was not likely to recover for twenty years at least. In any case it will never be the same Pakistan again. A continued ill will by Bangladesh against Pakistan would create

> innumerable problems. I had hopes that Bangladesh might one day, spearhead the Indian peace moves towards Pakistan and bring about a friendly understanding amongst these three South Asian states—Bangladesh, India and Pakistan—which would help make all the three strong politically, economically, and militarily to face the new threats that were gathering momentum all around us.

Biharis of Bangladesh and Mr Bhutto, the Prime Minister of Pakistan were two names that Sheikh Mujeeb hated most. They had done a lot of damage to his nation and he was determined to take revenge and to teach them a lesson. I pleaded with the Sheikh to give humane treatment to Biharis which he did but he was adamant about treating Mr Bhutto as his worst enemy. I kept on harping at the desirability of his opening a dialogue with Bhutto to settle some of the problems that plagued the two countries and were having their effect on the whole of South Asia. He would listen to me but never give an affirmative reply. Then one day suddenly I received a phone call from Lahore. Sheikh Mujeeb was on the line. He asked "Do you know what I have done today." I said, "Do tell me what you are up to now." He stunned me by saying "I have embraced Mr Bhutto on a public platform at Lahore. I know you would like that and therefore I am informing you first."

It brought tears to my eyes and I praised his farsightedness and statesmanship.

Lest my presence in Dacca gives Sheikh's enemies an opportunity to malign him for retaining a Sikh General in Dacca, I sought his permission to return to Delhi. Although he showed reluctance in the beginning, he finally agreed on the condition that he could consult me as and when necessary.

He wrote to me the following letter in response to a letter of mine:

> *My Dear General,*
>
> It was nice of you to have written me a delightful letter. Indeed it is very pleasant and interesting to hear from someone who is so dear and near to our heart. Your personal concern for my health and happiness, love and admiration for my children and, above all, your contributions to the cause of our liberation struggle have endeared you so much to all of us that we

can hardly forget you. We have been looking forward to seeing you here in the near future. Children always remember you respectfully. My wife joins me in sending you and your wife our warmest regards.

With kind thoughts.

Yours sincerely,
Sd. (Mujeeb)

Soon after this I received another call from the Sheikh. He said, "My son Jamal does not obey me or his mother. He can only be moulded by you for whom he has the highest respect. I propose to send him to you for further studies. Put him in any institution you like but keep him in your house and build up his character. I hope it is not too inconvenient for you or your wife."

I said, "Jamal is most welcome. Send him here and do not worry any more about him. He is a brave lad and will do well in life. He has been keen to get training as an Army officer. I shall try for his admission into the Indian Military Academy and send him to you as an officer for the Bangladesh Army."

He said, "That will be good."

On talking to the authorities concerned I discovered that Jamal could only be admitted into the IMA if he fulfilled certain educational qualifications. Bureaucracy made no exceptions. I was much depressed. Here was an opportunity to earn the gratitude of a powerful leader and we were so puny minded as not to avail of it.

I was saved from this predicament by Marshal Tito who visited Bangladesh and at the end of his visit asked Sheikh to send Jamal to the Yugoslav Academy for commissioning. Sheikh readily agreed and Jamal joined the Yugoslav Academy. He came to receive my blessings at our New Delhi home while on his way to Yugoslavia and was highly emotional.

He had to leave Yugoslav Academy because of language difficulty and was accepted in Sandhurst Academy by the British. Soon after Jamal joined the Bangladesh Army as a Commissioned Officer.

Alas this brave, innocent and promising lad had to die at the hands of an assassin along with the whole of his family including Sheikh Mujeeb.

Farewell to Friends

I was superannuated and was to retire on 2 January 1973 from service. It was a depressing day. I was mentally and physically fit at the age of 62 up to which I had been allowed to serve as an exceptional case, since 54 is the age of retirement for people of my seniority.

At this crucial moment we had a most powerful team of Secretaries in the Government of India who contributed immensely towards our historic victory. Mr T.N. Kaul, our Foreign Secretary, outshone everyone else in his ability and diplomatic aplomb. He could match the best in his line anywhere else in the world. Builders of nations like Kaul add lustre to the glory of the nations they represent at international meetings. Then there were Shri P.N. Haksar, later replaced by Mr P.N. Dhar the Principal Secretary to the Prime Minister with remarkable ability and wisdom based on high intellectual attainments. I took leave of all these magnificent men one by one.

A farewell dinner was arranged by my colleagues and friends and some of the highest officials including the Cabinet Secretary and Mr T.N. Kaul, the Secretary of External Affairs Ministry, attended. Mr R.N. Kao, in his beautiful English, eulogised my services and called me a "living legendary figure" and said that the Government would continue to avail of my services in some other capacity. Sure enough the Government employed me as an adviser in the Cabinet Secretariat immediately after retirement. I worked in that capacity for two years and then bade final good-bye to my colleagues.

Earlier a beautiful and touching poem named Salam (meaning "we salute thee') written by Mr B.B. Sabharwal of SSB in my honour was presented to me. It was a great pleasure to know the feelings of my colleagues and staff on my retirement in the shape of a sentimental poem.

I was then ushered into the room of Mrs Indira Gandhi, our Prime Minister, at my request, to bid her good-bye.

She was very gracious and highly appreciative of all I had done during my service, particularly in Bangladesh where, she said, "You were the backbone of all our success in Bangladesh." I felt well rewarded by these words at the termination of my service. I bowed to her while taking my leave. She bowed gracefully in response. And with that my Military Services came to an end.

Epilogue

Sheikh Mujeeb's Assassination Shocks the World

Whilst in America on a religious goodwill Mission, I learnt on 15 August 1975 that Sheikh Mujeeb had been assassinated along with his whole family including his two sons—Kamal and Jamal—with their wives and also his eight-year old son Russel, all of whom had fought for and suffered grievously in the Bangladesh War of Liberation. It shocked me so much that I returned to India at once.

It was a coup. Five misguided Majors of the Bangladesh Army had gunned down the whole unsuspecting family of Mujeeb, backed by the Tank Unit Commander, who brought his tanks out in the streets without any ammunition as a bluff ostensibly to put down an expected demonstration, but in actual fact to frighten the supporters of Mujeeb, and the bluff paid off.

All coups have a chain reaction. Mr Khondkar Mushtag Ahmad who became the President after lionising these Army mercenaries soon found himself displaced and so did his pro-Mujeeb successor. Never in history has there been a peaceful end to a selfish violent action.

Mujeeb was not just a perishable body. He represented an idea based on over forty years of political struggle in the subcontinent. He was a powerful leader of the Muslim League of Bengal. Later, he became a lieutenant of H.S. Suhrawardy and Fazlul Haq who had formed secular political parties, fully realising that communalism had no future.

This idea of Mujeeb which visualised democracy based on socialism and secularism although universally prevalent has been called Mujeebism by his admirers and has come to stay. It was for this idea that thousands of Hindus and Muslims of Bangladesh sacrificed their all including their lives. Ten million Hindus of Bangladesh cannot be happy to live in a 70 million strong Islamic state just as 65 million Muslims of India would feel uncomfortable if India became a Hindu theocratic state with its 650 million Hindus. Religion should cement relations and all religions should preach secular ideals in State matters. We are now about to enter the 21st century. Unfortunately lack of proper and widespread education still makes it possible for some power-hungry people to take advantage of simple, religiously emotional people, and foist the so-called religious Governments on them. But their days are numbered. People are becoming conscious of what is good or bad for them.

I visualise a prosperous Bangladesh. Its industrious and homogeneous population with enormous natural resources richly deserves this. The day is not far when the highly cultured and politically mature intelligentsia of Bangladesh will spearhead secular and socialist democratic movements in the developing world and would set an example for others to follow. I visualise a great mausoleum for the graves of Mujeeb and his dead family members in Dacca, treated with the same reverence with which great leaders of civilised countries are treated.

History would record the deeds of this great fighter for human rights in letters of gold. Bangladesh will never recover from its ills till it has shown due gratitude to its founder and the greatest martyr in its History, by honouring his memory and punishing those who killed him.

I have stated earlier the response I had from Sheikh Mujeeb when I had pointed out to him the weak security arrangements for his person. He loved his countrymen so much and had made such enormous sacrifices for their Independence that he could not dream of any Bangladeshi even thinking ill of him—much less assassinate him and his family members in cold blood. He paid the penalty for trusting too much, but his country lost the charismatic leader which history creates only once in several decades and therefore must suffer the consequences for a long time to come. There may be no dearth of powerful administrators or patriotic economists who would do their best to put this new Nation back on its own feet, but people are prepared to take the bitterest pill from the family physician they trust rather than the highly publicised medicine from the so-called experts. People like to see a halo around the heads of their political leaders, which only a long chain of sacrifices on the part of these leaders helps form.

The leadership and the people of India who had done so much for the establishment and stability of this new nation could only suffer the pain of this tragedy in silence. Instability in a weak neighbour attracts a lot of ills. Many other nations in the position of India would have felt justified to intervene in a situation where a whole nation was being held at ransom by a handful of assassins. It is for the suffering generations to say whether such unnatural calamities should be treated as the internal affairs of a Nation by friends and neighbours. Terrorism is assuming respectibility and is gaining recognition in world forums, which does not augur well for the future of our civilisation. It may be justified in some extreme cases but the reader would agree that Bangladesh is not such a case.

OPERATION EAGLE
CHITTAGONG HILL TRACTS

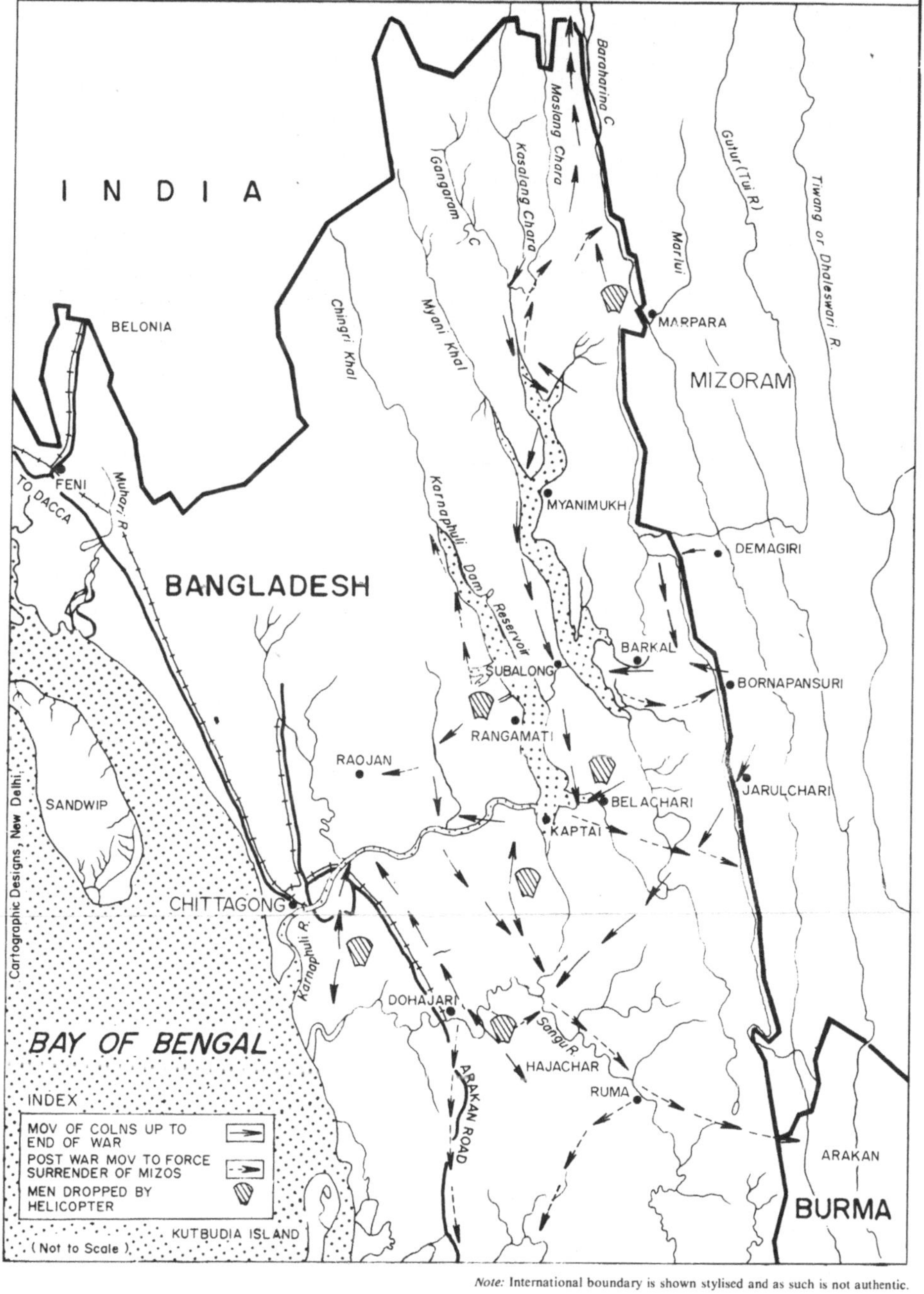

Note: International boundary is shown stylised and as such is not authentic.